W9-BMJ-785

SECOND EDITION

VOLUME FIVE
E. L. Konigsburg to A. A. Milne

Favorite Children's AUTHORS *and* ILLUSTRATORS

E. Russell Primm III, Editor in Chief

PO Box 326, Chanhassen, MN 55317-0326
800/599-READ
http://www.childsworld.com

A Note to Our Readers:

The publication dates listed in each author's or illustrator's selected bibliography represent the date of first publication in the United States.

The editors have listed literary awards that were announced prior to August 2006.

Every effort has been made to contact copyright holders of material included in this reference work. If any errors or omissions have occurred, corrections will be made in future editions.

Photographs: 8—E. L. Konigsburg; 12—Kathleen Krull; 16, 20, 108, 124, 132, 136, 140—Scholastic; 24—Kerlan Collection, University of Minnesota; 32—Hulton-Deutsch Collection / Corbis; 36—Marion Wood Kolisch / Harcourt; 40—Farrar, Straus, and Giroux; 44, 80, 104, 144—de Grummond Collection, University of Southern Mississippi; 48—Milan Sabatini / Scholastic; 52—HarperCollins; 56—Gillman and Soame / Kerlan Collection, University of Minnesota; 60—E. B. Lewis; 64—Riwkin Stockholm / Kerlan Collection, University of Minnesota; 68—Random House; 72—Marilyn Sanders / Simon & Schuster; 76—Karen Mohn; 84—Harcourt; 96—Judy B. Messer / HarperCollins; 112—Henry Holt; 120—Viking Press / Kerlan Collection, University of Minnesota; 128—Misha / Simon & Schuster; 148—Bachrach / HarperCollins; 152—Library of Congress.

An Editorial Directions book

Library of Congress Cataloging-in-Publication Data

Favorite children's authors and illustrators / E. Russell Primm III, editor-in-chief. — 2nd ed.
   v. cm.
  Includes bibliographical references and index.
  Contents: v. 1. Verna Aardema to Ashley Bryan.
  ISBN-13: 978-1-59187-057-9 (v.1 : alk. paper)
  ISBN-10: 1-59187-057-7 (v. 1 : alk. paper)
  ISBN-13: 978-1-59187-058-6 (v. 2 : alk. paper)
  ISBN-10: 1-59187-058-5 (v. 2 : alk. paper)
  ISBN-13: 978-1-59187-059-3 (v. 3 : alk. paper)
  ISBN-10: 1-59187-059-3 (v. 3 : alk. paper)
  ISBN-13: 978-1-59187-060-9 (v. 4 : alk. paper)
  ISBN-10: 1-59187-060-7 (v. 4 : alk. paper)
  ISBN-13: 978-1-59187-061-6 (v. 5 : alk. paper)
  ISBN-10: 1-59187-061-5 (v. 5 : alk. paper)
  ISBN-13: 978-1-59187-062-3 (v. 6 : alk. paper)
  ISBN-10: 1-59187-062-3 (v. 6 : alk. paper)
  ISBN-13: 978-1-59187-063-0 (v. 7 : alk. paper)
  ISBN-10: 1-59187-063-1 (v. 7 : alk. paper)
  ISBN-13: 978-1-59187-064-7 (v. 8 : alk. paper)
  ISBN-10: 1-59187-064-X (v. 8 : alk. paper)
  1. Children's literature—Bio-bibliography—Dictionaries—Juvenile literature. 2. Young adult literature Bio-bibliography—Dictionaries—Juvenile literature. 3. Illustrators—Biography—Dictionaries—Juvenile literature. 4. Children—Books and reading—Dictionaries—Juvenile literature. 5. Young Adults—Books and reading—Dictionaries—Juvenile literature. I. Primm, E. Russell, 1958–
  PN1009.A1F38 2007
  809'.8928203—dc22
  [B]   2006011358

First printing.

TABLE OF CONTENTS

MAJOR CHILDREN'S AUTHOR AND ILLUSTRATOR LITERARY AWARDS

THE AMERICAN BOOK AWARDS
Awarded from 1980 to 1983 in place of the National Book Award to give national recognition to achievement in several categories of children's literature

THE BOSTON GLOBE–HORN BOOK AWARDS
Established in 1967 by Horn Book *magazine and the* Boston Globe *newspaper to honor the year's best fiction, poetry, nonfiction, and picture books for children*

THE CALDECOTT MEDAL
Established in 1938 and presented by the Association for Library Service to Children division of the American Library Association to illustrators for the most distinguished picture book for children from the preceding year

THE CARNEGIE MEDAL
Established in 1936 and presented by the British Library Association for an outstanding book for children written in English

THE CARTER G. WOODSON BOOK AWARDS
Established in 1974 and presented by the National Council for the Social Studies for the most distinguished social science books appropriate for young readers that depict ethnicity in the United States

THE CORETTA SCOTT KING AWARDS
Established in 1970 in connection with the American Library Association to honor African American authors and illustrators whose books are deemed outstanding, educational, and inspirational

THE HANS CHRISTIAN ANDERSEN MEDAL
Established in 1956 by the International Board on Books for Young People to honor an author or illustrator, living at the time of nomination, whose complete works have made a lasting contribution to children's literature

THE KATE GREENAWAY MEDAL
Established by the Youth Libraries Group of the British Library Association in 1956 to honor illustrators of children's books published in the United Kingdom

THE LAURA INGALLS WILDER AWARD
Established by the Association for Library Service to Children division of the American Library Association in 1954 to honor an author or illustrator whose books, published in the United States, have made a substantial and lasting contribution to children's literature

THE MICHAEL L. PRINTZ AWARD
Established by the Young Adult Library Services division of the American Library Association in 2000 to honor literary excellence in young adult literature (fiction, nonfiction, poetry, or anthology)

THE NATIONAL BOOK AWARDS
Established in 1950 to give national recognition to achievement in fiction, nonfiction, poetry, and young people's literature

THE NEWBERY MEDAL
Established in 1922 and presented by the Association for Library Service to Children division of the American Library Association for the most distinguished contribution to children's literature in the preceding year

THE ORBIS PICTUS AWARD FOR OUTSTANDING NONFICTION
Established in 1990 by the National Council of Teachers of English to honor an outstanding informational book published in the preceding year

THE PURA BELPRÉ AWARD
Established in 1996 and cosponsored by the Association for Library Service to Children division of the American Library Association and the National Association to Promote Library Services to the Spanish Speaking to recognize a writer and illustrator of Latino or Latina background whose works affirm and celebrate the Latino experience

THE SCOTT O'DELL AWARD
Established in 1982 and presented by the O'Dell Award Committee to an American author who writes an outstanding tale of historical fiction for children or young adults that takes place in the New World

E. L. Konigsburg

Born: February 10, 1930

E. L. Konigsburg's books are funny, smart, and different. She has always said that she owes children a good story—and she delivers! She has written more than twenty books in the past thirty years and won just about every award you can name.

E. L. Konigsburg didn't start out to be a writer. She was born on February 10, 1930, in New York City. Her family moved often, and she grew up mostly in small mill towns in Pennsylvania. She read and drew a lot as a child and was an excellent student. No one in her family had ever graduated from college, but that didn't stop her. She earned her bachelor's degree

WHEN SHE WAS TEACHING CHEMISTRY AT A PRIVATE GIRLS' SCHOOL, E. L. KONIGSBURG REALIZED SHE WAS MORE INTERESTED IN WHAT WAS GOING ON INSIDE HER STUDENTS' HEADS THAN IN THEIR CHEMISTRY EXPERIMENTS.

in chemistry, got married, worked in a laboratory, went to graduate school, and taught science at a private girls' school.

Konigsburg had three children—Paul, Laurie, and Ross. She waited until all three were in school before becoming an author. She wrote in the morning while they were at school and read what she had written when they came home for lunch. They were a good audience—and a tough one! And since she had always loved painting, she also illustrated many of her books, using her children as models.

Konigsburg has written novels about modern children and novels about historic figures. But all of her books have some things in common. They are sharp and witty and filled with characters you remember. Most of the children in her books are searching for answers to the same basic questions: Who am I, and what makes me me? Am I normal? Am I weird? How am I like everyone else, and how am I different? Do I care if I'm different? Isn't it better to be me?

E. L. Konigsburg writes her books carefully. She usually spends a year to a year and a half on each book—and more if she has to do a lot of research.

"I try to let the telling be like fudge-ripple ice cream. You keep licking the vanilla, but every now and then you come to something darker and deeper and with a stronger flavor."

A PROUD TASTE FOR SCARLET AND MINIVER AND THE SECOND MRS. GIACONDA MIGHT BE CALLED HISTORICAL FANTASIES. THE FIRST BOOK IS ABOUT THE MEDIEVAL QUEEN ELEANOR OF AQUITAINE, AND THE OTHER FEATURES LEONARDO DA VINCI.

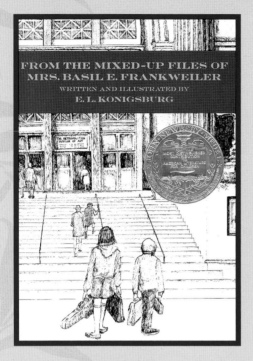

A Selected Bibliography of Konigsburg's Work

Outcast of 19 Schuyler Place (2004)

Silent to the Bone (2000)

The View from Saturday (1996)

Amy Elizabeth Explores Bloomingdale's (1992)

Samuel Todd's Book of Great Inventions (1991)

Samuel Todd's Book of Great Colors (1989)

Up From Jericho Tel (1986)

Journey to an 800 Number (1982)

Throwing Shadows (1979)

Father's Arcane Daughter (1977)

The Second Mrs. Giaconda (1975)

A Proud Taste for Scarlet and Miniver (1973)

About the B'nai Bagels (1969)

From the Mixed-Up Files of Mrs. Basil E. Frankweiler (1967)

Jennifer, Hecate, Macbeth, William McKinley, and Me, Elizabeth (1967)

Konigsburg's Major Literary Awards

1997 Newbery Medal
   The View from Saturday

1968 Newbery Honor Book
   Jennifer, Hecate, Macbeth, William McKinley, and Me, Elizabeth

1967 Newbery Medal
   From the Mixed-Up Files of Mrs. Basil E. Frankweiler

She writes and revises and erases and rewrites. She is very hard on herself because she thinks that writing for children demands excellence.

Besides her novels, Konigsburg has written and illustrated a number of picture books. Now that her children are all grown up, she sometimes uses her grandchildren as inspiration. She lives on the beach in north

> *"Finish. The difference between being a writer and being a person of talent is the discipline it takes to apply the seat of your pants to the seat of your chair and finish. Don't talk about doing it. Do it. Finish."*

Florida, and she loves to read and write and draw and paint. She also loves walking on the beach and going to movies. Whatever she does, she is always on the lookout for new ideas for books.

❧

WHERE TO FIND OUT MORE ABOUT E. L. KONIGSBURG

BOOKS

Kovacs, Deborah, and James Preller. *Meet the Authors and Illustrators: 60 Creators of Favorite Children's Books Talk about Their Work.* Vol. 1. New York: Scholastic, 1991.

McElmeel, Sharron L. *100 Most Popular Children's Authors: Biographical Sketches and Bibliographies.* Englewood, Colo.: Libraries Unlimited, 1999.

Rockman, Connie C., ed. *Eighth Book of Junior Authors and Illustrators.* New York: H. W. Wilson Company, 2000.

WEB SITES

EDUCATIONAL PAPERBACK ASSOCIATION
http://edupaperback.org/showauth.cfm?authid=251
To read an autobiographical sketch and booklist for E. L. Konigsburg

EDUPLACE
http://www.eduplace.com/kids/tnc/mtai/konigsburg.html
For biographical information about E. L. Konigsburg

WHEN A PUBLISHER WANTED TO REVISE A CHAPTER IN *FROM THE MIXED-UP FILES OF MRS. BASIL E. FRANKWEILER* THAT INVOLVED CHILDREN STANDING ON TOILET SEATS IN THE BATHROOM, KONIGSBURG REFUSED.

Kathleen Krull

Born: July 29, 1952

Kathleen Krull opens up world of information in her biographies and other books for young people. But she entertains her readers, too. Her books are often peppered with weird and comical facts about her subjects. She hopes this will help children to love reading as much as she did as a child.

Kathleen Krull was born in 1952 in Fort Leonard Wood, Missouri, and grew up in Wilmette, Illinois. As soon as she learned to read, she became an avid reader. The first book she read was Robert Louis Stevenson's *A Child's Garden of Verses*. Kathleen's weekly visit to the library was always a big event. As she later commented, "I thought books were the coolest thing in the world."

Kathleen's teachers encouraged her to write, too. She wrote her first little book, "A Garden Book," in second grade. As a fifth-grader,

---

KRULL IS MARRIED TO CHILDREN'S BOOK ILLUSTRATOR PAUL BREWER. HE ILLUSTRATED HER BOOKS *CLIP, CLIP, CLIP: THREE STORIES ABOUT HAIR* AND *HOW TO TRICK OR TREAT IN OUTER SPACE.*

she wrote "Hair-Do's and People I Know." In eighth grade, she wrote her first short story—"Death Waits Until after Dark." It was about a teacher who jumps out the window! Kathleen's own teacher gave her an A for the story, in spite of its frightful plot.

Kathleen loved books so much that, as a teenager, she worked part-time in the local library. Her love for reading got her into trouble, though. She was fired from her job because she spent her time reading instead of working.

Music was another big part of Kathleen's early years. She learned to play several musical instruments and began working as a church organist

A Selected Bibliography of Krull's Work

Isaac Newton (2006)

Leonardo da Vinci (2005)

The Boy on Fairfield Street: How Ted Geisel Grew Up to Become Dr. Seuss (2004)

How to Trick or Treat in Outer Space (2004)

A Woman for President (2004)

Harvesting Hope: The Story of Cesar Chavez (2003)

M Is for Music (2003)

Clip, Clip, Clip: Three Stories about Hair (2002)

Wilma Unlimited: How Wilma Rudolph Became the World's Fastest Woman (1996)

City within a City: How Kids Live in New York's Chinatown (1994)

Lives of the Musicians: Good Times, Bad Times (and What the Neighbors Thought) (1993)

Gonna Sing My Head Off! American Folk Songs for Children (1992)

It's My Earth, Too: How I Can Help the Earth Stay Alive (1992)

Songs of Praise (1989)

Sometimes My Mom Drinks Too Much (under the name Kevin Kenny, with Helen Krull, 1980)

Beginning to Learn about Shapes (with Richard L. Allington, 1979)

The Bugs Bunny Book (under the name Kathleen Cowles, 1975)

Krull's Major Literary Awards

2004 Carter G. Woodson Honor Book
2004 Pura Belpré Honor Book for Narrative
  Harvesting Hope: The Story of Cesar Chavez

1993 Boston Globe–Horn Book Nonfiction Honor Book
  Lives of the Musicians: Good Times, Bad Times (and What the Neighbors Thought)

> *"My 'hidden agenda' is always to create books that will mean as much to readers as books have meant to me."*

when she was twelve. She also taught piano to younger kids.

Krull graduated from Lawrence University in Appleton, Wisconsin, in 1974. For the next eleven years, she worked as an editor at several companies that publish children's books. These companies gave Krull her first taste of being a published author.

First, Krull joined Western Publishing Company in Racine, Wisconsin, as an associate editor. Western published her first book—*The Bugs Bunny Book*—in 1975. Krull became managing editor at Raintree Publishers in Milwaukee, Wisconsin, in 1979. There she wrote several books in the Beginning to Learn About series, with Richard L. Allington. These books explore basic concepts such as shapes, colors, and time. In 1982, Krull became a senior editor at Harcourt Brace Jovanovich in San Diego, California. Two years later, she quit her job to work as a full-time writer.

Krull loves writing biographies of famous people. In her entertaining Lives Of series, she writes about musicians, athletes, and U.S. presidents, to name a few. She is sure to include little-known, quirky facts about her subjects. For example, she had to mention that the composer Ludwig van Beethoven's favorite meal was macaroni and cheese!

KRULL PUBLISHED HER OWN PIANO ARRANGEMENTS OF FAVORITE CHRISTMAS CAROLS IN THE **1983** COLLECTION *THE CHRISTMAS CAROL SAMPLER.*

With her lifelong love of music, Krull has written several books that encourage music appreciation. In her World of My Own series, she explores different cities' ethnic communities. Krull follows the adventures of a girl named Alex in two fiction books. Her latest biography series, Giants of Science, began in 2005.

Today, Kathleen Krull works at her home in San Diego, California.

> *"One of [the] benefits [of being an author] is that I can't be fired. Especially for reading too much."*

❧

WHERE TO FIND OUT MORE ABOUT KATHLEEN KRULL

BOOKS
Graham, Paula, ed. *Speaking of Journals: Children's Book Writers Talk about Their Diaries.* Honesdale, Pa.: Boyds Mills Press, 1999.

Something about the Author. Vol. 106. Detroit: Gale, 1999

Silvey, Anita, ed. *The Essential Guide to Children's Books and Their Creators.* Boston: Houghton Mifflin Company, 2002.

WEB SITES
BOOK PAGE
http://www.bookpage.com/9605bp/childrens/kathleenkrull.html
To read an interview with Kathleen Krull

KATHLEEN KRULL
http://www.kathleenkrull.com
For a biography, a list of books, and links

AS A TEENAGER, KRULL WORKED SELLING DOUGHNUTS AND CUPCAKES IN A BAKERY.

Kathryn Lasky

Born: June 24, 1944

As a young girl, Kathryn Lasky was not interested in reading. "The truth was that I didn't really like the kind of books they had you reading at school," Lasky says. "So I made a voluntary withdrawal from reading in school." She did love the stories that her mother read to her at home. She also loved to make up her own stories. This love of storytelling inspired her to become an award-winning author of children's books. Lasky's best-known books for children include *The Night Journey, The Weaver's Gift, Pageant,* and *Double Trouble Squared.*

Kathryn Lasky was born on June 24, 1944, in Indianapolis, Indiana. When she was growing up, she was always thinking

---

LASKY'S BOOK *SUGARING TIME* WAS MADE INTO A VIDEO IN **1988.**

about stories. Sometimes she wrote down her stories; other times she just thought about stories. Other than the writing she did for school assignments, Kathryn did not share her stories. She did not share her writing with other people until she was much older.

Kathryn had always thought about being a writer, but she thought of writing as more of a hobby than a profession. It was not until she graduated from the University of Michigan that she thought about becoming a professional writer. She first worked as an English teacher. She also did some writing for magazines.

Lasky finally began sharing her writing with other people.

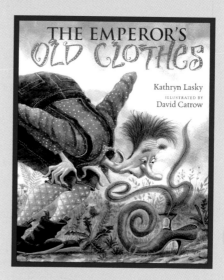

A Selected Bibliography of Lasky's Work

Born to Rule (2006)
Tumble Bunnies (2005)
American Spring (2004)
Before I Was Your Mother (2003)
The Man Who Made Time Travel (2002)
Baby Love (2001)
First Painter (2000)
The Emperor's Old Clothes (1999)
Alice Rose & Sam: A Novel (1998)
Cloud Eyes (1994)
Think Like an Eagle: At Work with a Wildlife Photographer (1992)
Double Trouble Squared (1991)
The Bone Wars (1988)
Pageant (1986)
Puppeteer (1985)
Sugaring Time (1983)
Jem's Island (1982)
The Night Journey (1981)
The Weaver's Gift (1980)
Tall Ships (1978)
Tugboats Never Sleep (1977)
Agatha's Alphabet, with Her Very Own Dictionary (1975)

Lasky's Major Literary Awards

2004 Orbis Pictus Honor Book
  The Man Who Made Time Travel

1984 Newbery Honor Book
  Sugaring Time

1981 Boston Globe–Horn Book Nonfiction Award
  The Weaver's Gift

She showed her stories to her parents and her husband. She continued to work on her writing while she worked as a teacher. Her first book, *Agatha's Alphabet, with Her Very Own Dictionary,* was published in 1975. Since that time, Lasky has written many other books, including nonfiction, historical fiction, and picture books.

Most of Lasky's writing has been nonfiction. She does a great deal of research on a topic before she begins writing. She tries to write about things that are interesting to young people. "In my own experience in writing nonfiction, I have always tried hard to listen, smell, and touch the place that I write about," Lasky says. She also writes books about her own experiences.

> *"When I was growing up I was always thinking up stories— whether I wrote them down or not didn't seem to matter. I was a compulsive story maker."*

Lasky enjoys writing many kinds of books for adults and young people. She has found that writing for young people is the most enjoyable. "I feel the same vulnerability that young people feel," Lasky notes. "When I was young, my mother used to tell me, 'People will say this is the best time of your life, but it's not. It's the worst.' Adolescence is a time of pain and anxiety, and stories come out of that tension. I seem to connect with that feeling pretty well."

———

LASKY USES HER MARRIED NAME, KATHRYN LASKY KNIGHT,
FOR HER ADULT BOOKS.

Lasky's husband, Christopher Knight, is a photographer and has provided photographs for several of her books. Lasky lives with her husband in Cambridge, Massachusetts. She continues to write for children, young people, and adults.

> *"I really do not care if readers remember a single fact. What I do hope is that they come away with a sense of joy."*

❧

WHERE TO FIND OUT MORE ABOUT KATHRYN LASKY

BOOKS

Kovacs, Deborah, and James Preller. *Meet the Authors and Illustrators: 60 Creators of Favorite Children's Books Talk about Their Work.* Vol. 2. New York: Scholastic, 1991.

Silvey, Anita, ed. *The Essential Guide to Children's Books and Their Creators.* Boston: Houghton Mifflin Company, 2002.

Something about the Author. Vol. 112. Detroit: Gale Research, 2000.

WEB SITES

KATHRYN LASKY HOME PAGE
http://www.kathrynlasky.com/
For biographical information about Kathryn Lasky and other activities

EDUPLACE
http://www.eduplace.com/kids/hmr/mtai/lasky.html
To read a biographical sketch of the author

LASKY'S FIRST NONFICTION BOOK WAS *TUGBOATS NEVER SLEEP.*

Patricia Lauber

Born: February 5, 1924

Patricia Lauber has a special gift: She makes science interesting and easy for kids to understand and enjoy. During a career that has spanned five decades, Patricia has penned more than eighty books. She has written about everything from penguins to planets, from the Ice Age to icebergs.

Patricia Lauber was born in New York City on February 5, 1924. As a child, Patricia loved listening to the stories that her mother read aloud to her. Patricia soon realized that, if she learned to read, she could have stories anytime she wanted. After she learned to read and

---

THE UNIVERSITY OF MINNESOTA HAS A COLLECTION OF PATRICIA LAUBER'S PAPERS. THEY INCLUDE MANUSCRIPTS, PROOFS, AND OTHER ITEMS CONNECTED WITH LAUBER'S BOOKS.

write, Patricia began creating her own tales and adventures. Everyone who read Patricia's stories loved them.

After graduating from college in 1945, Lauber knew what she wanted to do: be a writer. She returned to New York City, the capital of the publishing world. Her first job was as a writer for a magazine for grown-ups called *Look.* A year later, Patricia left *Look* to take a job as a writer and editor at *Junior Scholastic,* a newsmagazine for kids.

At Scholastic, Lauber wrote and edited stories for kids. While there, she also published her first book for children. The book, called *Magic Up Your Sleeve,* is nonfiction. In 1956, Lauber became the editor in chief of *Science World.* There, she began to perfect her skills as a science writer.

How does Lauber go about writing her books? First, she chooses a topic that interests her. Although Lauber has no training as a scientist, she is an excellent researcher. She makes sure that she has the most up-to-date information available on her subject. Finally, Lauber finds a way to share what she has learned with readers so they will understand the information and enjoy the book.

"Children are born curious, wanting and needing to understand the world around them, wanting to know why, how, and what: the very questions that scientists ask."

LAUBER MARRIED RUSSELL FROST III IN 1981. THEY LIVE IN CONNECTICUT.

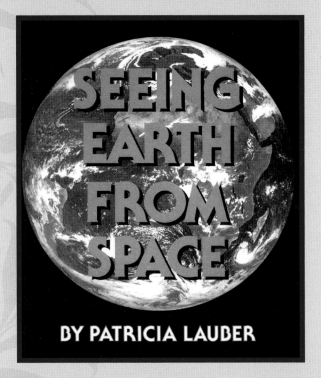

BY PATRICIA LAUBER

A Selected Bibliography of Lauber's Work

What You Never Knew about Beds, Bedrooms & Pajamas (2005)

The True-or-False Book of Dogs (2003)

What You Never Knew about Tubs, Toilets & Showers (2001)

Purrfectly Purrfect: Life at the Acatemy (2000)

The Tiger Has a Toothache (1999)

Flood: Wrestling with the Mississippi (1996)

Be a Friend to Trees (1994)

Alligators: A Success Story (1993)

Seeing Earth from Space (1990)

The News about Dinosaurs (1989)

Volcano: The Eruption and Healing of Mount St. Helens (1986)

Seeds Pop, Stick, Glide (1980)

What's Hatching Out of that Egg? (1979)

Everglades Country: A Question of Life or Death (1973)

Your Body and How It Works (1962)

Clarence, the TV Dog (1955)

Lauber's Major Literary Awards

1991 Orbis Pictus Honor Book
   Seeing Earth from Space

1990 Orbus Pictus Honor Book
   The News about Dinosaurs

1987 Newbery Honor Book
   Volcano: The Eruption and Healing of Mount St. Helens

Throughout Lauber's career, a number of her books have been singled out for special awards. Her books have been chosen as New York Academy of Sciences Honor Books as well as Newbery Honor Books. Lauber has also received several awards for her lifetime contributions to children's literature.

What makes Lauber's science books so special? Lauber believes that, like fiction, a good science book has a story line. She makes her story lines interesting and exciting, so that kids will want to know what

"I was born wanting to write."

happens next. Lauber also carefully selects illustrations to accompany and explain her words.

Lauber also writes fiction for kids. Her best-known fiction books are the five Clarence books. The title character is a lovable dog based on Lauber's own dog named Clarence. One day, Lauber told a friend a silly story about her dog. The friend enjoyed the tale, and recommended that Lauber write it down. Lauber did, and the first of the Clarence books, *Clarence, the TV Dog,* was born.

When Lauber isn't researching and writing her next book, she likes to travel. She has been all over the United States and Europe. Lauber's trips sometimes spark new ideas for her writing.

❧

WHERE TO FIND OUT MORE ABOUT PATRICIA LAUBER

BOOKS

Silvey, Anita, ed. *The Essential Guide to Children's Books and Their Creators.*
Boston: Houghton Mifflin Company, 2002.

Sutherland, Zena. *Children and Books.*
New York: Addison Wesley Longman, 1997.

WEB SITE
HOUGHTON MIFFLIN: MEET THE AUTHOR
http://www.eduplace.com/kids/hmr/mtai/lauber.html
To read a biographical sketch and booklist for Patricia Lauber

---

LAUBER SAYS THAT MOST OF HER FICTION BOOKS ARE BASED
ON DOGS OR HORSES SHE HAS KNOWN.

Robert Lawson

Born: October 4, 1892
Died: May 26, 1957

When Robert Lawson was growing up in Montclair, New Jersey, his family lived in a house that used to belong to famous painter George Innes. Lawson's room was Innes's old studio. Even so, it was a long time before Lawson decided to become an artist.

"I did not, as a child, have any particular interest in drawing and did none until my last year in high school, when it was pointed out to me that I must prepare to do something in the world," he wrote years later.

Robert Lawson was born on October 4, 1892. In the early 1910s, he attended what is now called the Parsons School of Design in New York City. Then he set out to establish himself as an artist, designing ads and stage sets and producing illustrations

---

THE STORY OF FERDINAND WAS CONTROVERSIAL WHEN IT WAS PUBLISHED JUST BEFORE THE BEGINNING OF WORLD WAR II (1939–1945). SOME PEOPLE THOUGHT IT WAS A PACIFIST STORY, AGAINST ALL WAR. IN GERMANY, ADOLF HITLER BANNED FERDINAND.

for newspapers and magazines. In 1922, Lawson married Marie Abrams, an author and illustrator. The two bought a house in Connecticut, and then spent three years paying for it by designing greeting cards at the rate of one a day. Lawson illustrated his first children's book, *The Wonderful Adventures of Little Prince Toofat* by George Randolph Chester, in 1922. But he was unhappy with the quality of the printed book, so he didn't do any more for quite a while.

The Lawsons eventually returned to New York. They felt they had lost touch with the publishing world, and it was probably true. When Lawson got his next book to illustrate, he learned that the editor would

A Selected Bibliography of Lawson's Work

Adam of the Road (1970)

The Spring Rider (1968)

The Story of Simpson and Sampson (1968)

The Great Wheel (1957)

The Tough Winter (1954)

Rabbit Hill (1944)

They Were Strong and Good (1940)

Ben and Me: A New and Astonishing Life of Benjamin Franklin as Written by His Good Mouse Amos (1939)

The Sword in the Stone (Illustrations only, 1939)

Mr. Popper's Penguins (Illustrations only, 1938)

Wee Gillis (Illustrations only, 1938)

Four & Twenty Blackbirds (Illustrations only, 1937)

The Story of Ferdinand (Illustrations only, 1936)

Wee Men of Ballywooden (Illustrations only, 1930)

The Wonderful Adventures of Little Prince Toofat (Illustrations only, 1922)

Lawson's Major Literary Awards

1958 Newbery Honor Book
   The Great Wheel

1945 Newbery Medal
   Rabbit Hill

1941 Caldecott Medal
   They Were Strong and Good

1939 Caldecott Honor Book
   Wee Gillis

1938 Caldecott Honor Book
   Four & Twenty Blackbirds

> "My mother taught me to like good books. She never forbade my reading trashy books or the funny papers; she didn't care what I read, as long as I was reading something."

have given it to him earlier, but he thought Lawson was dead.

That book was Arthur Mason's *Wee Men of Ballywooden,* and Lawson's whimsical drawings attracted attention. He was hired to illustrate more of Mason's books and soon was spending most of his time on children's books.

Many of the books Lawson illustrated in the 1930s are forgotten today, but some are still read, such as Richard and Florence Atwater's *Mr. Popper's Penguins* and *The Sword in the Stone* by T. H. White. Perhaps his best-known book was *The Story of Ferdinand,* published in 1936. The story about a bull who would rather smell flowers than fight was written by Lawson's friend Munro Leaf and became a classic.

Lawson soon started writing his own books. The first was *Ben and Me: A New and Astonishing Life of Benjamin Franklin as Written by His Good Mouse Amos,* a look at the life of Benjamin Franklin through the eyes of a mouse. (Lawson eventually wrote more of these history-through-animals books. One was narrated by Paul Revere's horse, another by Christopher Columbus's parrot.) Lawson liked history. His book *They Were Strong and Good* tells the story of his own family. It won the

WHEN MUNRO LEAF FIRST SHOWED ROBERT LAWSON HIS STORY ABOUT FERDINAND THE BULL, LAWSON THOUGHT IT WAS FUNNY, BUT HE DIDN'T WANT TO ILLUSTRATE IT. "I HAD NEVER DRAWN A BULL IN MY LIFE," HE SAID.

Caldecott Medal for illustration. Lawson also wrote stories about the animals that lived near his house. One of them, *Rabbit Hill,* won the Newbery Medal. Lawson was the first writer/artist to win both the Newbery and the Caldecott Medals.

Lawson died in 1957. Fifty years later, his books are still attracting new young readers.

> *"I have never, as far as I can remember, given one moment's thought as to whether any drawing that I was doing was for adults or children. I have never changed one conception or line or detail to suit the supposed age of the readers."*

WHERE TO FIND OUT MORE ABOUT ROBERT LAWSON

BOOKS

McElmeel, Sharron L. *100 Most Popular Children's Authors: Biographical Sketches and Bibliographies.*. Englewood, Colo.: Libraries Unlimited, 1999.

Sutherland, Zena. *Children and Books.*
New York: Addison Wesley Longman, 1997.

WEB SITES

BUD PLANET
http://www.bpib.com/illustrat/lawson.htm
To read a biographical sketch of Robert Lawson

THE SCOOP
http://friend.ly.net/users/jorban/biographies/lawsonrobert/index.html
For a biographical sketch and booklist for Robert Lawson

LAWSON'S MOTHER BELIEVED IN GOOD BOOKS. HER WORD FOR THE OTHER KIND WAS "SCULCH."

Munro Leaf

Born: December 4, 1905
Died: December 21, 1976

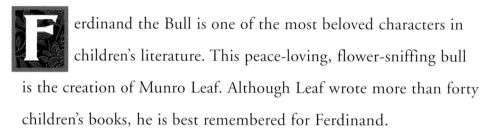

Ferdinand the Bull is one of the most beloved characters in children's literature. This peace-loving, flower-sniffing bull is the creation of Munro Leaf. Although Leaf wrote more than forty children's books, he is best remembered for Ferdinand.

Wilbur Munro Leaf was born in Hamilton, Maryland, in 1905. When he was a baby, his family moved to Washington, D.C. Little is known about his early life, but he later claimed to have had "a very happy childhood." He attended public schools in Washington, D.C., and later enrolled in the University of Maryland in College Park.

Leaf worked hard during summer vacations, holding jobs as a road construction worker, rancher, and steamship deckhand. In 1926, while he was still in college, he married Margaret Butler Pope. They eventually had two sons, Andrew and James.

After graduation in 1927, Leaf enrolled in Harvard University in Cambridge, Massachusetts. He earned a master's degree in English

---

DURING WORLD WAR II, LEAF WORKED WITH THEODORE GEISEL (ALSO KNOWN AS DR. SEUSS) TO PRODUCE A MANUAL FOR THE TROOPS ABOUT THE DISEASE MALARIA.

literature 1931. While pursuing his graduate studies, he worked as a high school English teacher and football coach.

In 1932, Leaf began a job as an editor at the Frederick A. Stokes publishing company in New York City. One day in 1934, he was riding the city's subway. Sitting nearby was a mother who was trying to explain to her child why not to use the word *ain't*. That gave Leaf the idea for his first children's book, *Grammar Can Be Fun*. He illustrated it himself with whimsical stick figures.

Leaf published his best-known book, *The Story of Ferdinand*, in 1936. It's the tale of a gentle Spanish bull named Ferdinand who likes to sit around sniffing flowers under a tree rather than take part in bullfights. Published during the Spanish Civil War (1936–1939), the book unleashed a flurry of controversy. Many people believed the book had hidden meanings. They were sure Leaf wrote it to further certain political ideas. But Leaf insisted that it was just an animal story. He chose a bull, he explained, because there were already so many stories about dogs, cats, rabbits, and mice.

Leaf's friend Robert Lawson illustrated *The Story of Ferdinand*, and the two collaborated again

> *"The reading that you do . . . will help to make you the kind of person you want to be when you're grown up."*
> —from Leaf's
> **Reading Can Be Fun**

GERMAN DICTATOR ADOLF HITLER ORDERED ALL COPIES OF *THE STORY OF FERDINAND* TO BE BURNED BECAUSE HE SAW THE BOOK AS A POLITICAL STATEMENT PROMOTING PEACE AND DEMOCRACY.

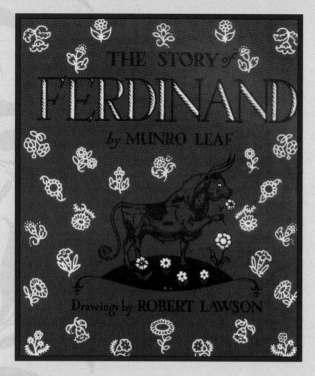

A Selected Bibliography of Leaf's Work

Metrics Can Be Fun! (1976)

Who Cares? I Do (1971)

Being an American Can Be Fun (1964)

Science Can Be Fun (1958)

Reading Can Be Fun (1953)

Arithmetic Can Be Fun (1949)

A War-Time Handbook for Young Americans (1942)

The Watchbirds: A Picture Book of Behavior (1939)

Wee Gillis (Text only, 1938)

Noodle (1937)

The Story of Ferdinand (Text only, 1936)

Grammar Can Be Fun (1934)

on the 1938 book *Wee Gillis.* This picture book about an orphan boy in Scotland proved to be very popular. Leaf went on to write a handful of books illustrated by other people. But he was also the author of more than thirty children's books that he illustrated himself. Many are simple teaching books that deal with subjects such as manners, safety, history, geography, patriotism, and science.

Leaf joined the U.S. Army in 1942 and served in World War II (1939–1945). After the

"Since no such thing as an illiterate democracy can exist, books as the backbone of education are vitally important abroad."

war, he worked on several projects for the U.S. government. From 1961 to 1964, the U.S. State Department sent him and his wife on cultural and educational tours. They visited twenty-four countries, speaking to teachers and students about democratic ideals, literacy, and children's books. This experience inspired Leaf to write a booklet on tolerance titled *I Hate You! I Hate You!* He later called it his most satisfying project.

Leaf died at his home in Garrett Park, Maryland, at the age of seventy-one.

WHERE TO FIND OUT MORE ABOUT MUNRO LEAF

BOOKS

Berger, Laura Standley, ed. *Twentieth-Century Children's Writers*. 4th ed. Detroit: St. James Press, 1995.

Silvey, Anita, ed. *The Essential Guide to Children's Books and Their Creators*. Boston: Houghton Mifflin Company, 2002.

WEB SITES

CHILDREN'S LITERATURE NETWORK
http://www.childrensliteraturenetwork.org/brthpage/12dec/12-4leaf.html
For a biography of this author and illustrator

ENCYCLOPAEDIA BRITANNICA
http://www.britannica.com/ebi/article-9314782
For a biography of Munro Leaf

IN 1938, WALT DISNEY STUDIOS MADE *THE STORY OF FERDINAND* INTO A SHORT ANIMATED FILM CALLED *FERDINAND THE BULL*, WHICH WON AN ACADEMY AWARD.

Edward Lear

Born: May 12, 1812
Died: January 29, 1888

Edward Lear wrote poetry and created illustrations more than one hundred and fifty years ago. His work is still read by children throughout the world, and many of his poems are being published with new illustrations even today. He wrote many poems, nonsense songs, and stories for children. His best-known book is *The Owl and the Pussycat.*

Edward Lear was born into a wealthy family on May 12, 1812, in London, England. His father was a stockbroker. When Edward was about four years old, his father lost a lot of money from his stocks.

LEAR HAD TWENTY BROTHERS AND SISTERS.

The family had to give up their wealthy lifestyle. Edward was sent to live with his sister Ann. She was twenty-one years older than he was and served as his mother. Edward never knew his real mother well.

Edward was not a healthy child. When he was about five years old, it was discovered that he had epilepsy, a disease of the central nervous system. He suffered from asthma and had poor eyesight. He also experienced severe mood changes. Edward was often depressed as a young boy. His childhood was not happy.

Edward Lear started to make a living as an artist when he was fifteen years old. He drew sketches of the human body and sold them to medical students for their studies. He also made money by teaching other people how to draw.

When Edward Lear was eighteen years old, he illustrated a book about parrots for the city zoo. He was hired by the earl of Derby to create a collection of drawings of rare birds. Working on the collection allowed him to travel to Italy and Greece to sketch birds that he saw.

Lear was also asked to entertain the earl of Derby's grandchildren. He wrote nonsense limericks and other poems that he shared with the children. In 1846, he added illustrations to the verses and published his first book, *A Book of Nonsense.* He continued to write verse and published several other collections of poems and limericks.

———

IN 1846, LEAR GAVE DRAWING LESSONS TO ENGLAND'S QUEEN VICTORIA!

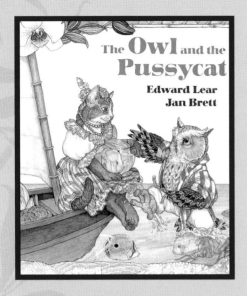

A Selected Bibliography of Lear's Work

A New Nonsense Alphabet (1988)
Lear in the Original (1975)
The Quangle Wangle's Hat (1969)
The Owl and the Pussycat (1953)
A Nonsense Alphabet (1952)
The Complete Nonsense of Edward Lear (1947)
The Complete Nonsense Book (1912)
Nonsense Songs and Stories (1895)
More Nonsense Pictures, Rhymes, Botany, and Alphabets (1871)
A Book of Nonsense (1846)

Lear's Major Literary Award

1999 Boston Globe–Horn Book Picture Book Honor Book
  The Owl and the Pussycat

Even though he is best known as a children's author, Lear was a very good painter. He studied at famous art schools and traveled throughout Europe studying art. He created many drawings, oil paintings, and watercolor paintings during his life. There are large collections of his paintings in galleries and museums in England.

> "Henceforth, let the inhabitants of the world be divided into two classes—them as has seen the Taj Mahal and them as hasn't."

After his years of traveling, Edward Lear settled in San Remo, Italy.

He died there on January 29, 1888. He was seventy-five years old.

᪇

WHERE TO FIND OUT MORE
ABOUT EDWARD LEAR

BOOKS
Kamen, Gloria. *Edward Lear, King of Nonsense: A Biography.*
New York: Atheneum Books, 1990.

Lewis, J. Patrick. *Boshblobberbosh: Runcible Poems for Edward Lear.*
New York: Harcourt, Brace, 1998.

Silvey, Anita, ed. *The Essential Guide to Children's Books and Their Creators.*
Boston: Houghton Mifflin Company, 2002.

WEB SITES
EDWARD LEAR HOME PAGE
http://www.nonsenselit.org/Lear/
For a biographical sketch of Edward Lear, a booklist, and a selection of his art

THE KNITTING CIRCLE
http://www.sbu.ac.uk/~stafflag/edwardlear.html
To read a biographical sketch of and a booklist for Edward Lear

---

LEAR DID NOT USE HIS OWN NAME WHEN HE PUBLISHED HIS FIRST BOOK,
A BOOK OF NONSENSE. INSTEAD, HE USED THE NAME DERRY DOWN DERRY.

Ursula K. Le Guin

Born: October 21, 1929

Throughout her long career, Ursula K. Le Guin has consistently enjoyed shattering stereotypes. It was believed that only men could write science fiction. She quickly became one of the most popular and well respected science fiction writers of all time. It was also believed that science fiction writers couldn't write "serious" novels. Again, Le Guin established herself as a true literary novelist.

She was born Ursula Kroeber on October 21, 1929, in Berkeley, California. Her father was an anthropologist who founded the anthropology department at the University of California at Berkeley. Her mother, Theodora Kroeber, was an author best known for her children's books, including *The Inland Whale* and *Ishi in Two Worlds: A Biography of the Last Wild Indian in North America.*

Growing up with such talented and intellectual parents, Ursula was constantly surrounded by books, and her young

LE GUIN BELIEVES THAT ANY AUTHOR WHO WANTS TO WRITE FANTASY SHOULD USE J. R. R. TOLKIEN'S LORD OF THE RINGS SERIES AS A MODEL.

mind was always stimulated. Her curiosity and imagination grew rapidly. She recalls sitting around listening to grown-ups talk about "really interesting stuff." She soon began writing her own stories.

The first story Ursula submitted for publication was a science-fiction tale about time travel. She sent it to a popular science-fiction magazine. The story was rejected. Ursula was just eleven years old at the time. She was not discouraged and continued to write.

In 1947, she left California to attend Radcliffe College in Cambridge, Massachusetts. She then went to Columbia University in New York City for her master's degree. In 1953, she was aboard the ocean liner the *Queen Mary* on her way to study in France when she met Charles Le Guin. They married a few months later in Paris.

Returning to the United States, the Le Guins lived first in Macon, Georgia, and then settled in Portland, Oregon, where they still reside. Le Guin never stopped writing, turning out stories and poetry.

> *"It's my job to listen for ideas, and welcome them when they come, and do something with them. I'm not saying it's easy. But there's nothing I'd rather do."*

After seven years of rejection letters, she had the same story accepted by both a literary magazine and *Amazing Stories,* a science fiction magazine. The tale, called "April in Paris," tells the story of figures from different historical

A VERY VERSATILE WRITER, URSULA K. LE GUIN HAS WRITTEN NOVELS, NOVELLAS, SHORT STORIES, POETRY, ESSAYS, TRANSLATIONS OF OTHER WRITERS' WORKS, AND CHILDREN'S BOOKS.

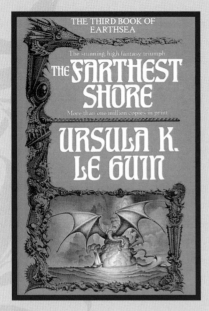

A Selected Bibliography of Le Guin's Work

Incredible Good Fortune (2006)

Tom Mouse (2002)

Other Wind (2001)

Telling (2000)

Jane on Her Own: A Catwings Tale (1999)

Wonderful Alexander and the Catwings (1994)

A Ride on the Red Mare's Back (1992)

Catwings Return (1989)

Catwings (1988)

The Farthest Shore (1972)

The Tombs of Atuan (1971)

A Wizard of Earthsea (1968)

Rocannon's World (1966)

Le Guin's Major Literary Awards

1972 National Book Award
  The Farthest Shore

1972 Newbery Honor Book
  The Tombs of Atuan

1969 *Boston Globe–Horn Book* Fiction Award
  A Wizard of Earthsea

periods who travel to fifteenth-century Paris to meet and marry. The literary magazine offered no money; *Amazing Stories* offered her thirty dollars for her story. She chose the science fiction publication.

"Thirty dollars meant a lot to us back then," she explains. And so she began reading a lot of science fiction and working on improving her writing in the genre. Ursula K. Le Guin's first novel was *Rocannon's World,* published in 1966. Other novels, novellas, and short stories followed. In 1968, she published the first book in her Earthsea trilogy, *A Wizard of Earthsea. The Tombs of Atuan* and *The Farthest Shore* followed, completing one of the most beloved fantasy trilogies of all time. Like much of her work, this trilogy features strong female characters, breaking yet another stereotype in the science fiction and fantasy genres.

Ursula K. Le Guin is proud of the fact she has brought science fiction to many new readers. "I do seem to be someone who has carried people across from realistic literature to fantasy and science fiction, and back," she explains. "I'm happy to do that. If I'm a stepping stone, walk on me, for heaven's sake." It's a walk her loyal readers are thrilled to take.

❧

WHERE TO FIND OUT MORE ABOUT URSULA K. LE GUIN

BOOKS

Reid, Suzanne Elizabeth. *Presenting Ursula Le Guin.* New York: Twayne Publishers, 1997.

Rockman, Connie C., ed. *The Ninth Book of Junior Authors and Illustrators.* New York: H. W. Wilson Company, 2004.

Sutherland, Zena. *Children and Books.* New York: Addison Wesley Longman, 1997.

WEB SITES

LE GUIN'S WORLD

http://hem.passagen.se/peson42/lgw/bio.html
For a biographical sketch of Ursula K. Le Guin and a link to a booklist

URSULA K. LE GUIN HOME PAGE

http://www.ursulakleguin.com/Bio.html
To read a biographical sketch of Ursula K. Le Guin

―――

ALTHOUGH MANY OF HER STORIES TAKE PLACE IN THE FUTURE IN FARAWAY ALIEN WORLDS, URSULA K. LE GUIN ADDRESSES MANY OF THE SAME SUBJECTS AS REALISTIC FICTION, SUCH AS HUMAN NATURE, POLITICS, AND FEELINGS.

Madeleine L'Engle

Born: November 29, 1918

Madeleine L'Engle does not have many happy memories of her school days. She attended a boarding school in Switzerland, where she felt that she did not fit in. Instead of paying attention in school, she thought about a poem or a story she was writing. Her interest in writing continued throughout her life. L'Engle has published plays, poems, and novels for both children and adults. Her most popular books for children include the Time Fantasy series and the Austin Family series.

Madeleine L'Engle was born on November 29, 1918, in New York City. Her mother was a pianist and her father was a journalist. Her parents had many friends who were artists, writers, and musicians. Madeleine was surrounded by creative people who encouraged her to use her imagination. She was always writing stories and poems. She wrote her first stories when she was five years old.

L'ENGLE'S REAL NAME IS MADELEINE FRANKLIN, BUT SHE ALWAYS USES
THE NAME L'ENGLE FOR HER WRITING.

When she was twelve years old, Madeleine and her family moved to Europe. They lived in France and Switzerland. Madeleine was a shy girl and felt like an outsider at her Swiss boarding school. Writing was much more important to Madeleine than school was.

Madeleine and her family returned to the United States so she could attend high school. She enjoyed school much more as a student in Charleston, South Carolina.

After graduating from high school, Madeleine L'Engle attended Smith College. She studied English and continued to work on her creative writing. She graduated in 1941 and moved to New York City.

A Selected Bibliography of L'Engle's Work

Ordering of Love: The New and Collected Poems of Madeleine L'Engle (2005)

Genesis Trilogy (2001)

The Other Dog (2001)

Full House: An Austin Family Christmas (1999)

Miracle on 10th Street & Other Christmas Writings (1998)

Troubling a Star (1994)

The Glorious Impossible (1990)

Many Waters (1986)

A Ring of Endless Light (1980)

A Swiftly Tilting Planet (1978)

A Wind in the Door (1973)

The Young Unicorns (1968)

The Arm of the Starfish (1965)

The Moon by Night (1963)

A Wrinkle in Time (1962)

Meet the Austins (1960)

L'Engle's Major Literary Awards

1981 Newbery Honor Book
  A Ring of Endless Light

1980 American Book Award
  A Swiftly Tilting Planet

1963 Newbery Medal
  A Wrinkle in Time

> *"The world is changing rapidly— that terrifies people. We know a great deal more now about the nature of the universe than we used to, which I think makes it all the more exciting. But change is frightening to people. And when you get frightened, you strike out."*

In New York, L'Engle worked as an actor in theater productions. She also had time to write. She published her first two novels while living in New York. She also met an actor named Hugh Franklin and married him in 1946. The couple later had three children.

L'Engle and her family moved to Connecticut. She and her husband owned a general store. Operating the store and raising her children kept L'Engle busy. She did not have much time to write. She could concentrate on her writing only at night when the house was quiet. The family eventually moved back to New York City. Her husband continued his acting career. L'Engle began to find great success as a writer.

L'Engle's most popular children's book is *A Wrinkle in Time*. The book was rejected by twenty-six publishers before it was published in 1962.

> *"I had to write. I had no choice in the matter. It was not up to me to say I would stop, because I could not. It didn't matter how small or inadequate my talent. If I never had another book published . . . I still had to go on writing."*

L'ENGLE HAS BEEN THE LIBRARIAN AT THE CATHEDRAL CHURCH OF ST. JOHN THE DIVINE IN NEW YORK CITY FOR MORE THAN THIRTY YEARS.

Many publishers thought the book was too difficult for young readers. It turned out to be very popular and led to four other books in the Time Fantasy series.

L'Engle has won many awards for her books. She lives in New York City and continues to write books for both young people and adults.

❧

WHERE TO FIND OUT MORE ABOUT MADELEINE L'ENGLE

BOOKS

Chase, Carole F. *Madeleine L'Engle, Suncatcher: Spiritual Vision of a Storyteller.* San Diego, Calif.: LuraMedia, 1995.

Gonzales, Doreen. *Madeleine L'Engle: Author of* A Wrinkle in Time. New York: Macmillan, 1991.

Kovacs, Deborah, and James Preller. *Meet the Authors and Illustrators: 60 Creators of Favorite Children's Books Talk about Their Work.* Vol. 1. New York: Scholastic, 1991.

Rockman, Connie C., ed. *The Ninth Book of Junior Authors and Illustrators.* New York: H. W. Wilson Company, 2004.

WEB SITES

AMAZON.COM: A CONVERSATION WITH MADELEINE L'ENGLE
http://www.amazon.com/exec/obidos/ts/feature/6238/002-6906564-3054408
To read an interview with Madeleine L'Engle

EDUCATIONAL PAPERBACK ASSOCIATION
http://edupaperback.org/showauth.cfm?authid=59
To read an autobiographical sketch of and a booklist for Madeleine L'Engle

———

A MOVIE-PRODUCTION COMPANY PURCHASED THE RIGHTS TO THE FIRST THREE BOOKS IN L'ENGLE'S TIME FANTASY SERIES. THE MOVIE VERSION OF *A WRINKLE IN TIME* AIRED IN 2004.

Lois Lenski

Born: October 14, 1893
Died: September 11, 1974

Growing up in a small town was an important part of Lois Lenski's life. Her experiences and memories of growing up can be seen in her books. Lenski illustrated more than fifty books for other authors. She wrote and illustrated more than 100 of her own books. She also wrote poetry, plays, and songs for children herself. Her books for children and young people include *Cowboy Small, Grandmother Tippytoe, Strawberry Girl,* and *Indian Captive: The Story of Mary Jemison.*

Lois Lenski was born on October 14, 1893, in Springfield, Ohio. Her father was the pastor of a church. When she was

LENSKI BELIEVED THAT CHILDREN'S BOOKS SHOULD DO MORE THAN ENTERTAIN. SHE WANTED THEM TO "ILLUMINE THE WHOLE ADVENTURE OF LIVING."

six years old, Lois and her family moved to Anna, Ohio, a small rural town. Lois loved her life in this community. "It offered all a child could enjoy and comprehend," she later noted. "Commonplace and ordinary, it had no particular beauty or grace, but it soon became my own."

Learning was important in Lois's family. Her parents encouraged her to read and to work hard in school. They wanted their children to be able to go to college. Lois read many books and also liked to draw. She would spend hours copying pictures from books and magazines.

> *"I have a strong urge to work, I am not happy unless I am at work. I believe this compulsion to work was not only a part of my conscious training, but also a part of my Polish inheritance."*

The town of Anna was so small it did not have a high school. Lois had to take a train each day to a nearby town to attend high school. She graduated in 1911, and her family then moved to Columbus, Ohio. Lois Lenski enrolled as a student at Ohio State University, where she studied to be a teacher. She also took classes in drawing and art. When Lenski graduated, her parents thought she would become a teacher. She instead took the advice of one of her art professors. She moved to New York City to study at the Art Students League.

THE DAVY SERIES WAS BASED ON LENSKI'S GRANDSON, DAVID, WHO LIVED WITH HER DURING THREE SUMMER VACATIONS.

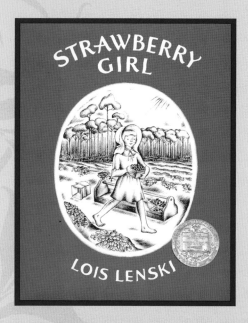

A Selected Bibliography of Lenski's Work

Chimney Corner Stories: Tales for Little Children (Illustrations only, 1992)

Sing a Song of People (1987)

Debbie and Her Pets (1971)

City Poems (1971)

Debbie Goes to Nursery School (1970)

High-Rise Secret (1966)

Davy Goes Places (1961)

Cowboy Small (1949)

Judy's Journey (1947)

Strawberry Girl (1945)

Bayou Suzette (1943)

Indian Captive: The Story of Mary Jemison (1941)

Phebe Fairchild, Her Book (1936)

Grandmother Tippytoe (1931)

Skipping Village (1927)

Lenski's Major Literary Awards

1946 Newbery Medal
  Strawberry Girl

1942 Newbery Honor Book
  Indian Captive: The Story of Mary Jemison

1937 Newbery Honor Book
  Phebe Fairchild, Her Book

She studied for four years and took part-time jobs to support herself. She worked on lettering greeting cards and drawing fashion advertisements. She met an artist named Arthur Covey and helped him paint his murals. After a trip to Europe to study art, she returned to New York and married Covey.

In 1918, Lenski was hired to illustrate the *Children's Frieze Book.* She went on to illustrate more books for other

"My poems are the very essence, the fabric behind all my work for children. The themes in them are my life's blood. They are my legacy to the children I love."

authors including the Betsy Tacy series by Maud Hart Lovelace. Lenski published her first book, *Skipping Village,* in 1927. Many of Lenski's books have a historical focus. She often used fictional characters in her books to tell real stories.

Lenski continued writing throughout the 1950s and 1960s. A number of manuscripts were published after her death. Lenski died at her home in Florida on September 11, 1974.

❧

WHERE TO FIND OUT MORE ABOUT LOIS LENSKI

BOOKS

Lenski, Lois. *Journey into Childhood: The Autobiography of Lois Lenski.*
Philadelphia: Lippincott, 1972.

Sutherland, Zena. *Children and Books.*
New York: Longman, 1997.

WEB SITES

MILNER LIBRARY: ILLINOIS STATE UNIVERSITY
http://www.mlb.ilstu.edu/ressubj/speccol/lenski/Welcome.html
To read a biographical sketch of and a booklist for Lois Lenski

PURPLE HOUSE PRESS
http://www.purplehousepress.com/sig/lenskibio.htm
To read a biographical sketch of Lois Lenski

———

THE BOOK *COWBOY SMALL* WAS ADAPTED INTO
A MOTION-PICTURE SCREENPLAY IN **1955.**

Julius Lester

Born: January 27, 1939

There is a historical voice running through the writing of Julius Lester. "It's a storytelling voice," he explains, "a southern voice, an older voice, the voice of somebody who certainly has long memories. It's a voice inside me, a voice I know very well. It's an amalgam of my father's voice and all kinds of voices

that I heard throughout my growing up." It is certainly a voice beloved by readers both young and old.

Julius Lester was born on January 27, 1939, in St. Louis, Missouri, the son of a Methodist minister. When Julius was two years old, he and his family moved to Kansas. By the time he was in high school, they had settled in Nashville, Tennessee. Julius spent most of his summers as a child at his grandmother's farm in Arkansas.

LESTER'S ADVICE FOR YOUNG WRITERS IS TO READ AS MUCH AS POSSIBLE, LEARN GRAMMAR, AND CONSTANTLY REWRITE. HE BELIEVES THAT THE WAY YOU WRITE SOMETHING THE FIRST TIME IS RARELY THE BEST THAT IT CAN BE.

Growing up in the American South in the 1940s and 1950s, Julius witnessed first-hand the effects of segregation and racism. His experiences led to his involvement in the civil rights movement of the 1960s, after his graduation from Fisk University in 1960.

During this period, Julius Lester wrote songs, sang, and played the guitar, the banjo, the clarinet, and the piano. He even recorded two albums of his own songs. Becoming friends with Pete Seeger, a leader of the emerging folk music scene, Lester collaborated on a book with Seeger entitled *The 12-String Guitar As Played by Leadbelly.* This book was an instructional manual based on the work of the

A Selected Bibliography of Lester's Work

Cupid (2007)

Time's Memory (2006)

Day of Tears (2005)

Shining (2003)

Pharaoh's Daughter: A Novel of Ancient Egypt (2002)

Ackamarackus: Julius Lester's Sumptuously Silly Fantastically Funny Fables (2001)

What a Truly Cool World (1999)

Black Cowboy, Wild Horses: A True Story (1998)

Sam and the Tigers: A New Telling of Little Black Sambo (1996)

Othello: A Novel (1995)

John Henry (1994)

The Last Tales of Uncle Remus (1994)

Further Tales of Uncle Remus (1990)

How Many Spots Does a Leopard Have? And Other Tales (1989)

More Tales of Uncle Remus: Further Adventures of Brer Rabbit, His Friends, Enemies, and Others (1988)

The Tales of Uncle Remus (1987)

This Strange New Feeling (1982)

The Knee-High Man, and Other Tales (1972)

Long Journey Home: Tales from Black History (1972)

Two Love Stories (1972)

Black Folktales (1969)

To Be a Slave (1968)

Lester's Major Literary Awards

2005 Coretta Scott King Award
   Day of Tears

1995 Boston Globe–Horn Book Picture Book Award
   John Henry

1988 Coretta Scott King Author Honor Book
   The Tales of Uncle Remus

1983 Coretta Scott King Author Honor Book
   This Strange New Feeling

1969 Newbery Honor Book
   To Be a Slave

legendary blues and folk musician Leadbelly. It was also Lester's first published work.

As Lester got more involved with the civil rights movement, he applied his love of photography to recording key events in the movement. His photos are now part of the Smithsonian Institution and document this important period in U.S. history. Lester also wrote many books for adults about black history, politics, and civil rights.

"I am not sure what led me to become a writer. There was no decision. Rather there was a growing certainty that grew from the age of seventeen until I was twenty-one that this was what I was supposed to do with my life."

During this time, Lester produced and hosted a radio program on WBAI-FM, a noncommercial radio station in New York City, that served as the voice of many emerging political movements in the 1960s. He also produced a program on WNET, New York public radio.

"I write because the lives of all of us are stories. If enough of those stories are told, then perhaps we will begin to see that our lives are the same story. The differences are merely in the details."

Lester's publisher urged him to write children's books. His first book for young readers was *To Be a Slave*. It asked readers to imagine what it was like to be a slave. Three of Lester's great-grandparents had been slaves, and the need to learn more about his personal past led him to

---

In addition to recording two albums of original songs, Lester performed with folk music greats Pete Seeger, Phil Ochs, and Judy Collins.

study the subject. His next book for children, *Black Folktales,* also explored African American history, folklore, and politics.

Lester continues to write books for both adults and children based on his own family history and the history of African Americans. "Sometimes I feel like there are all these spirits of blacks inside me, people who never had the opportunity to tell their stories, and they have chosen me to be their voice." His readers are fortunate to have the chance to listen to those voices.

❧

WHERE TO FIND OUT MORE ABOUT JULIUS LESTER

BOOKS

Fogelsong, Marilee. *Lives and Works: Young Adult Authors.* Danbury, Conn.: Grolier, 1999.

Hill, Christine M. *Ten Terrific Authors for Teens.* Berkeley Heights, N.J.: Enslow, 2000.

Lester, Julius. *On Writing for Children and Other People.* New York: Dial Books, 2004.

Rockman, Connie C., ed. *Eighth Book of Junior Authors and Illustrators.*
New York: H. W. Wilson Company, 2000.

WEB SITES
CHILDRENS LITERATURE
http://www.childrenslit.com/f_lester.html
To read an autobiographical sketch of Julius Lester

EDUPLACE
http://www.eduplace.com/kids/tnc/mtai/lester.html
To read a biographical sketch of Julius Lester

———

LESTER WRITES TWO TO THREE HOURS A DAY WHEN HE
IS BEGINNING A BOOK, AND ALMOST NONSTOP WHEN HE NEARS THE END.
HIS MAJOR DISTRACTION IS PLAYING CARD GAMES ON THE COMPUTER.

Gail Carson Levine

Born: September 17, 1947

Gail Carson Levine grew up in a creative family. Her father wrote stories in his spare time and her mother wrote plays for her students to perform. Her sister became a painter and an art professor. For many years, Gail was interested in drawing and painting too. Then she discovered a character named Ella, and a storyteller was born!

She was born Gail Carson on September 17, 1947, in New York City. Her father owned an art studio, and her mother was a teacher. Although Gail was always jotting down stories and poems

LEVINE HAS WRITTEN MANY OF HER STORIES ON THE TRAIN, RIDING BACK AND FORTH TO WORK IN NEW YORK CITY.

at school, she never seriously thought about being a writer. Instead, she wanted to be an actor or a painter.

She went to City College of the City University of New York. And in 1967, she married David Levine. She graduated from college in 1969 and went to work for the New York State Department of Labor. Later, she worked for the Department of Commerce and the Department of Social Services. Her jobs included helping people find work and improve their lives.

> *"Many people are cursed with obedience and with attending too much to other people's expectations."*

Gail Carson Levine's interest in the theater led to her first published work. She and her husband wrote *Spacenapped,* a musical play for children. The play was produced by a neighborhood theater in Brooklyn, New York.

Later, Levine took some painting classes and became interested in the stories behind the pictures. She wrote several picture books, and a novel based on her father's childhood experiences growing up in an orphanage. Although the picture books were never published, they helped Levine see how much fun it could be to tell a story with words.

During the late 1980s, Levine was looking for a story to write for another class. She had trouble thinking of a plot, so she decided to focus on the story of Cinderella. But she wanted her character to

---

WHEN SHE WAS A CHILD, LEVINE'S FAVORITE BOOK WAS
PETER PAN BY J. M. BARRIE.

A Selected Bibliography of Levine's Work

Fairest (2006)
Princess Tales (2003)
Betsy Who Cried Wolf (2002)
Cinderellis and the Glass Hill (2000)
The Wish (2000)
Dave at Night (1999)
The Fairy's Mistake (1999)
Princess Sonora and the Long Sleep (1999)
The Princess Test (1999)
Ella Enchanted (1997)

Levine's Major Literary Awards

1998 Newbery Honor Book
   Ella Enchanted

> *"I love when I surprise myself and come up with something unexpected."*

be more rebellious and less of a Goody Two-shoes than the fairy-tale Cinderella. That story became Levine's first published novel, *Ella Enchanted*. The book was published in 1997 and was named a Newbery Honor Book.

Levine continued to work fairy tales into her stories and published several stories featuring traditional fairy-tale characters. She also revised her early novel about her father's childhood. It was published as *Dave at Night* in 1999.

Levine and her husband live in an old farmhouse in

Brewster, just north of New York City, along with their Airedale dog. She continues to spin marvelous stories that mix fairy tales and reality and charm readers everywhere.

∾

WHERE TO FIND OUT MORE ABOUT GAIL CARSON LEVINE

BOOKS

Levine, Gail Carson. *Writing Magic: Creating Stories that Fly.* New York: Collins, 2006.

Rockman, Connie C., ed. *Eighth Book of Junior Authors and Illustrators.* New York: H. W. Wilson Company, 2000.

Wilson, Kathleen, ed. *Major 20th Century Writers: A Selection of Sketches from Contemporary Authors.* Vol. 4. Detroit: Gale Research, 1999.

WEB SITES

HARPERCHILDRENS.COM
http://www.harperchildrens.com/hch/author/author/levine/index.asp
To read a biographical sketch of Gail Carson Levine and the transcript of an interview with the author

KIDSREADS.COM
http://www.kidsreads.com/authors/au-levine-gail-carson.asp
To read an autobiographical sketch with the author

———

AS A CHILD, LEVINE ENJOYED READING BECAUSE IT GAVE HER QUIET TIME AWAY FROM HER PARENTS AND OLDER SISTER.

C. S. Lewis

Born: November 29, 1898
Died: November 22, 1963

C. S. Lewis was a literary critic, religious writer, poet, and science fiction novelist. Most of his writing was for an adult audience. But Lewis is also remembered as a children's author. He wrote the Chronicles of Narnia series. The series begins with *The Lion, the Witch and the Wardrobe* and includes six additional titles.

Clive Staples (C. S.) Lewis was born on November 29, 1898, in Belfast, Ireland. "Jack," as he was nicknamed, was surrounded by books as a young child. He was a good student and did well in school. He spent most of his time reading books and writing stories. When Jack was ten years old, his mother became sick and died.

LEWIS DIED ON THE SAME DAY THAT
PRESIDENT JOHN F. KENNEDY WAS ASSASSINATED.

Jack and his brother were not close to their father. After their mother's death, they were sent to boarding school, where Jack did not have pleasant experiences. He had a hard time concentrating on his studies. After a while, Jack's father hired a teacher to tutor him. The tutor helped Jack focus on his studies and prepared him for college.

Lewis first attended Oxford University in 1916. After less than a year at Oxford, he joined the British army and was sent to France. He was wounded during fighting in World War I (1914–1918). He returned to England to recover from his injuries. Once he was healthy, he continued his studies.

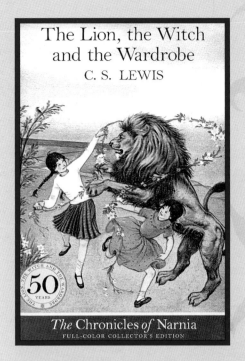

A Selected Bibliography of Lewis's Work
The Last Battle (1956)
The Magician's Nephew (1955)
The Horse and His Boy (1954)
The Silver Chair (1953)
The Voyage of the Dawn Treader (1952)
Prince Caspian (1951)
The Lion, the Witch and the Wardrobe (1950)

Lewis's Major Literary Award
1956 Carnegie Medal
  The Last Battle

Lewis went on to teach English and philosophy at Magdalen College at Oxford University. He also wrote poetry and scholarly books. Lewis developed a strong Christian religious belief. Most of his books and writings emphasized this strong belief.

> *"Reality, in fact, is always something you couldn't have guessed. That's one of the reasons I believe Christianity. It's a religion you couldn't have guessed."*

During the 1930s, Lewis began meeting with a group of Christian writers. This group was called "The Inklings," and one member was J. R. R. Tolkien. The group met once a week. At the meetings, members of the group would read their writings and then have discussions. This group was an important part of Lewis's life.

After writing many novels, religious works, and poetry for adults, Lewis began work on the Chronicles of Narnia during the 1950s. He wrote the books as a way to share ideas that interested him. He wanted readers of the books to share his own beliefs in the Christian faith.

Many people thought the series included too much violence and was not appropriate for children. "A number of mothers, and still more, schoolmistresses, have decided that it is likely to frighten children, so it is not selling very well," Lewis noted. "But the real children

IN 1979, CBS AIRED AN ANIMATED VERSION OF *THE LION, THE WITCH AND THE WARDROBE*. IN 1989, PBS AIRED THE MINISERIES *THE CHRONICLES OF NARNIA*.

like it, and I am astonished how some very young ones seem to understand it. I think it frightens some adults, but very few children." This series went on to become very popular and is still read by children today.

The Chronicles of Narnia was the only series that Lewis wrote for children. Lewis died on November 22, 1963. A writer for the *Times Literary Supplement* noted that "for the last thirty years of his life no other Christian writer in this country had such influence on the general reading public as C. S. Lewis."

❧

WHERE TO FIND OUT MORE ABOUT C. S. LEWIS

BOOKS

Gormley, Beatrice. *C. S. Lewis: Christian and Storyteller.*
Grand Rapids, Mich.: Eerdmans Books for Young Readers, 1998.

Sibley, Brian. *The Land of Narnia: Brian Sibley Explores the World of C. S. Lewis.*
New York: Harper & Row, 1990.

Stone, Elaine Murray. *C. S. Lewis: Creator of Narnia.* New York: Paulist Press, 2001.

WEB SITES

INTO THE WARDROBE
http://cslewis.drzeus.net/
To read two biographical sketches of C. S. Lewis and book information

NARNIA FROM HARPERCOLLINS
http://www.narnia.com/
For information on the books in the Chronicles of
Narnia series and an interactive tour of Narnia

―――

THE CHRONICLES OF NARNIA WAS RELEASED AS A MAJOR MOTION PICTURE IN 2005.

E. B. Lewis

Born: December 16, 1956

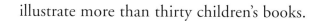

In the art world, E. B. Lewis is a well-respected watercolor artist. His work hangs in art galleries throughout the United States. Fortunately for the literary world, he has also used his talent to illustrate more than thirty children's books.

Lewis's illustrations add a rich dimension to any story he approaches. Using vibrant, shimmering colors, he paints intimate scenes with realistic details. The sensitive facial expressions of his characters capture their complex emotions and moods.

Earl Bradley Lewis was born in Philadelphia, Pennsylvania, in 1956. As a child, Earl tended to be a troublemaker. But he learned to direct his energies toward a more creative outlet—art. He began to show artistic talent at an early age. Luckily, he had family members for inspiration. Two of his uncles were artists, and he decided to be one, too.

LEWIS SERVES ON THE BOARD OF DIRECTORS OF THE PHILADELPHIA WATERCOLOR CLUB.

> *"My books basically deal with very tough situations—issues of death and loss and love and friendship."*

One of Earl's uncles ran the School Art League at Philadelphia's Temple University. After Earl finished sixth grade, he began taking art classes there on Saturday mornings. In this setting, he started his formal art training under Philadelphia artist Clarence Wood.

In 1975, Lewis enrolled in Temple University's Tyler School of Art. There he majored in graphic design and illustration, studying art education as well. As his training progressed, he found that watercolor was the medium that suited him best.

As soon as he graduated in 1979, Lewis began teaching art and doing freelance painting and graphic design. His fine-art paintings soon attracted attention. Philadelphia art galleries started exhibiting his work, and when they held art shows, his paintings sold out.

When Lewis was first asked to illustrate a children's book, he was not sure he wanted to do it. Then he took a close look at some children's books. He realized that they contained some of the finest art he had seen. He was convinced that illustration was a great way to use his talents.

Lewis's first illustrated book—*Fire on the Mountain*, by Jane Kurtz—came out in 1994. The story is a traditional Ethiopian folktale,

---

LEWIS TEACHES ILLUSTRATION AT THE UNIVERSITY OF THE ARTS IN PHILADELPHIA.

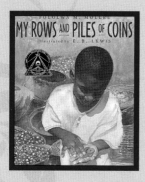

A Selected Bibliography of Lewis's Work

Night Boat to Freedom (2006)

This Little Light of Mine (2005)

Coming On Home Soon (2004)

Talkin' about Bessie: The Story of Aviator Elizabeth Coleman (2002)

The Other Side (2001)

Dirt on Their Skirts (2000)

Little Cliff and the Porch People (1999)

The Magic Tree: A Folktale from Nigeria (1999)

My Rows and Piles of Coins (1999)

Virgie Goes to School with Us Boys (1999)

The Bat Boy and His Violin (1998)

The Jazz of Our Street (1998)

I Love My Hair! (1997)

Only a Pigeon (1997)

Magid Fasts for Ramadan (1996)

Down the Road (1995)

The New King (1995)

Fire on the Mountain (1994)

Lewis's Major Literary Awards

2005 Caldecott Honor Book
   Coming On Home Soon

2003 Coretta Scott King Illustrator Award
   Talkin' about Bessie: The Story of Aviator Elizabeth Coleman

2001 Coretta Scott King Illustrator Honor Book
   Virgie Goes to School with Us Boys

2000 Coretta Scott King Illustrator Honor Book
   My Rows and Piles of Coins

1999 Coretta Scott King Illustrator Honor Book
   The Bat Boy and His Violin

and Lewis went on to illustrate several more books with African themes. *The New King* is a folktale from Madagascar, and *The Magic Tree* is from Nigeria. *My Rows and Piles of Coins* takes place in modern-day Tanzania.

Only a Pigeon is the heartwarming story of a boy in Ethiopia who tenderly raises his pet pigeons. In preparing his illustrations, Lewis spent five weeks in Ethiopia observing local people, scenes, and daily life.

Many of Lewis's illustrated books are stories about African American children learning to find their own strength. For

"Some of the best artwork in the country is being done in children's books."

example, *I Love My Hair!* shows a little girl celebrating her wonderful head of hair. *Little Cliff and the Porch People* portrays a boy's rich experiences in an African American community in the Mississippi Delta during the 1950s.

Lewis lives in Folsom, New Jersey, where he continues to work on his paintings. He enjoys visiting schools and talking to kids about art.

∾

WHERE TO FIND OUT MORE ABOUT E. B. LEWIS

BOOKS

McElmeel, Sharron L. *Children's Authors and Illustrators Too Good to Miss: Biographical Sketches and Bibliographies*. Englewood, Colo: Libraries Unlimited, 2004.

Rockman, Connie C. *Eighth Book of Junior Authors and Illustrators*.
New York: H. W. Wilson, 2000.

Silvey, Anita, ed. *The Essential Guide to Children's Books and Their Creators*.
Boston: Houghton Mifflin Company, 2002.

WEB SITES

CHILDREN'S LITERATURE NETWORK
http://www.childrensliteraturenetwork.org/brthpage/12dec/12-16lewis.html
To read a biography of the artist

E. B. LEWIS
http://www.eblewis.com/default2.asp
For a biography of Earl Bradley Lewis, a listing of his books, current information, and visits

———

A 1993 ISSUE OF *THE ARTISTS' MAGAZINE* RAN A COVER STORY ON LEWIS. THE ARTICLE CAUGHT THE ATTENTION OF A CHILDREN'S BOOK PUBLISHER, AND THIS LED TO HIS CAREER AS AN ILLUSTRATOR.

Astrid Lindgren

Born: November 14, 1907
Died: January 28, 2002

Pippi Longstocking is a famous book character. Her wild red braids make her easy to recognize. Children love reading about her zany life. Pippi is the invention of children's author Astrid Lindgren. Lindgren wrote many books during her life. She is best known for the Pippi Longstocking books.

She was born Astrid Ericsson on November 14, 1907, in Vimmerby, Sweden. Astrid had an older brother and two younger sisters. Her parents were farmers. She once said that she couldn't imagine anyone having more fun than she did growing up.

Astrid remembered what it was like to discover books and to learn to read. "Country girls like me didn't have books . . . after a while I learned how to read myself and I was constantly on the hunt for more books to satisfy my hunger for reading. . . . My first book was *Snow White* with

---

PIPPI LONGSTOCKING HAS BEEN TRANSLATED INTO SIXTY-TWO LANGUAGES.

on the cover a drawing of a chubby little princess with black curls," Lindgren once said.

In high school, her friends often told her they thought she would be an author one day. Astrid didn't like to hear that. "I think that scared me, I didn't dare try, even though somewhere deep inside I probably thought it would be fun to write," she explained.

In 1923, after graduating from high school, she worked for the Vimmerby newspaper. Then, in 1926, she moved to the city of Stockholm, Sweden, to study to be a secretary. Over the next ten years, she married Sture Lindgren and had two children, Lars and Karin.

"It is useless to make a conscious effort to try and recall how things were. You have to relive your own childhood and remember with your very soul what the world looked like."

Astrid Lindgren's children loved hearing their mother's stories about her childhood and growing up on the farm. When Karin was seven, she became ill with pneumonia. She begged her mother to tell her a story. A name popped into Karin's head. "Tell me a story about Pippi Long-stocking!" she begged. So Lindgren did. Lindgren and Karin made up many stories about the zany girl named Pippi. But none of them was ever written down.

Three years later, Lindgren fell and broke her ankle. She had to stay in bed for two weeks, and she needed something to do. She decided to

THERE IS A BRONZE STATUE OF ASTRID LINDGREN IN A PARK IN STOCKHOLM. THE NAME OF THE PARK IS TENERLUNDEN.

A Selected Bibliography of Lindgren's Work

Most Beloved Sister (2002)
Pippi Longstocking in the Park (2001)
Pippi to the Rescue (2000)
Pippi Goes to the Circus (1999)
Pippi Goes to School (1998)
Lotta's Easter Surprise (1991)
Ronia, the Robber's Daughter (1983)
Emil's Pranks (1971)
The Tomten and the Fox (1966)
The Tomten (1961)
Pippi Longstocking (1950)

Lindgren's Major Literary Award

1958 Hans Christian Andersen Medal for Authors

write down the Pippi stories they had been inventing. Two months later, Lindgren gave Karin the stories for her tenth birthday.

Lindgren decided to send her Pippi stories to writing contests. A year later, *Pippi Longstocking* won first prize. Lindgren's career as an author had begun. *Pippi Longstocking* was published in the United States in 1950. For the next fifty years, Lindgren continued to write children's stories. She wrote the screenplays for movies based on her books. She was also active in politics, and she worked to make the world more peaceful.

Lindgren received many awards for her children's books. *Pippi Longstocking* continued receiving awards fifty years after it was published. Lindgren died on January 28, 2002. She will be remembered as one of the best-loved children's authors.

> *"I don't write books for children. I write books for the child I am myself. I write about things that are dear to me—trees and houses and nature—just to please myself."*

WHERE TO FIND OUT MORE ABOUT ASTRID LINDGREN

BOOKS

Hurwitz, Johanna. *Astrid Lindgren: Storyteller to the World.* New York: Viking Kestrel, 1989.

McElmeel, Sharron L. *100 Most Popular Children's Authors: Biographical Sketches and Bibliographies.* Englewood, Colo.: Libraries Unlimited, 1999.

Metcalf, Eva Maria. *Astrid Lindgren.* New York: Twayne Publishers, 1995.

Silvey, Anita, ed. *The Essential Guide to Children's Books and Their Creators.* Boston: Houghton Mifflin Company, 2002.

WEB SITES

ASTRID LINDGREN HOME PAGE
http://www.astridlindgrensworld.com/
To read information about Astrid Lindgren

CHILDREN'S AUTHORS PAGES
http://falcon.jmu.edu/~ramseyil/lindgren.htm
For a photo and a biographical sketch of Astrid Lindgren

———

TODAY, THERE IS AN AMUSEMENT PARK IN SWEDEN NAMED "ASTRID LINDGREN'S WORLD." IT IS DEDICATED TO LINDGREN AND HER BOOKS. CHILDREN FROM ALL OVER THE WORLD VISIT THE PARK.

Leo Lionni

Born: May 5, 1910
Died: October 12, 1999

If Leo Lionni had never written a single book, he still would have been a famous man. In his long career, Lionni was a painter, an architecture critic, and a professor of design. He was the art director of several important magazines, which means that he decided how they would look and what sort of pictures they would contain. He displayed his art in galleries and museums in the United States and Europe. Yet when Leo Lionni died and the newspapers wrote about him, the first thing most of them said was that he wrote books for children.

Leo Lionni was born on May 5, 1910, in Amsterdam, the Netherlands. His family was artistic and creative. Leo's mother was an opera singer. He had an uncle who was an architect. Two other uncles were art collectors. They made sure that Leo saw good art.

In school, Leo was mostly interested in nature and art. He kept terrariums filled with animals and plants. He also liked to go to the art museum and copy the pictures and sculptures he saw there.

EVEN THOUGH THE CHARACTERS IN LIONNI'S *LITTLE BLUE AND LITTLE YELLOW* ARE JUST BLOBS OF COLOR, LIONNI SAID CHILDREN ALWAYS GUESS RIGHT WHEN ASKED WHICH BLOB IS LITTLE BLUE'S MOTHER AND WHICH ONE IS HIS FATHER.

The Lionni family moved several times during Leo's childhood, and he lived in Belgium, the United States, and Italy. He returned to the United States to live in 1939 and became a U.S. citizen in 1945.

Leo Lionni's first book for children was written almost by accident. In 1958, he was taking his two grandchildren on a train trip from New York to Connecticut. The children were restless, and their grandfather

"I was not a great reader. I don't remember any children's books. I remember books about expeditions to the North Pole and to the South Pole, and I remember reading about penguins."

A Selected Bibliography of Lionni's Work

An Extraordinary Egg (1994)

On My Beach There Are Many Pebbles (1994)

A Busy Year (1992)

Mr. McMouse (1992)

Matthew's Dream (1991)

Nicolas, Where Have You Been? (1987)

It's Mine! (1986)

Colors to Talk about (1985)

Letters to Talk about (1985)

Numbers to Talk about (1985)

Words to Talk about (1985)

Cornelius: A Fable (1983)

Let's Make Rabbits: A Fable (1982)

Geraldine, the Music Mouse (1979)

In the Rabbitgarden (1975)

Pezzettino (1975)

The Greentail Mouse (1973)

Theodore and the Talking Mushroom (1971)

Fish Is Fish (1970)

Alexander and the Wind-Up Mouse (1969)

The Alphabet Tree (1968)

The Biggest House in the World (1968)

Frederick (1967)

Tico and the Golden Wings (1964)

Swimmy (1963)

Inch by Inch (1960)

Little Blue and Little Yellow: A Story for Pippo and Ann and Other Children (1959)

Lionni's Major Literary Awards

1970 Caldecott Honor Book
Alexander and the Wind-Up Mouse

1968 Caldecott Honor Book
Frederick

1964 Caldecott Honor Book
Swimmy

1961 Caldecott Honor Book
Inch by Inch

"*I have a theory that it's impossible not to think in words, and it's impossible not to think in images. I believe we think in both, and it's very difficult to keep them apart. I've tried to do that, and it's like jumping your own shadow.*"

tried to entertain them. He tore circles of colored paper from a magazine and made up a story about a little blue blob and a little yellow blob who were friends. The children (and the other passengers!) were delighted. Lionni made his story into a mock-up book

and showed it to a book editor. In 1959, it was published as *Little Blue and Little Yellow: A Story for Pippo and Ann and Other Children.* Lionni had begun a new career.

In the 1950s, Little Blue and Little Yellow was unusual. For one thing, its characters were neither people nor animals. They were just blobs. For another, it was created by using collage, an art technique that was unusual in books then.

Lionni created a book almost every year for the rest of his life. Two of his most famous are *Swimmy* and *Frederick*. In *Swimmy*, a school of small red fish fool a big tuna that wants to eat them by making themselves look like an even bigger fish. Swimmy, a little black

CHILDREN LOVE HIS BOOKS, BUT LIONNI ALWAYS HAD A HARD TIME GETTING ALONG WITH CHILDREN HIMSELF. "I DON'T KNOW HOW TO GET TO THEM," HE EXPLAINED. "I WISH I COULD JUST READ TO THEM."

fish, becomes the eye of the make-believe big fish. *Frederick,* like many of Lionni's books, is about a mouse. The plot is a bit like Aesop's fable of the ants and the grasshopper. Frederick the mouse is a poet who helps his friends through the winter with his stories and songs. Art helps the group survive.

Lionni continued to write and paint until the end of his life. He died on October 12, 1999, in Italy.

&

WHERE TO FIND OUT MORE ABOUT LEO LIONNI

BOOKS

Lionni, Leo. *Between Worlds: An Autobiography of Leo Lionni.*
New York: Knopf, 1997.

Silvey, Anita, ed. *The Essential Guide to Children's Books and Their Creators.*
Boston: Houghton Mifflin Company, 2002.

Smaridge, Norah. *Famous Author-Illustrators for Young People.*
New York: Dodd, Mead, 1973.

WEB SITE

RANDOM HOUSE
http://www.randomhouse.com/kids/lionni/
To read biographical information about Leo Lionni

———

LIONNI DIDN'T THINK CHILDREN'S BOOKS SHOULD BE JUST FOR CHILDREN. "I BELIEVE A GOOD CHILDREN'S BOOK SHOULD APPEAL TO ALL PEOPLE WHO HAVE NOT COMPLETELY LOST THEIR ORIGINAL JOY AND WONDER IN LIFE," HE SAID.

Myra Cohn Livingston

Born: August 17, 1926
Died: August 23, 1996

As a young girl, Myra Cohn Livingston learned how to play the French horn. She was very good at playing it and thought about becoming a professional musician. Instead, she decided to become a writer and a teacher. She published more than forty books of poetry and stories for children. She was also the editor of several books of poetry for children. Livingston's best-known books include *Wide Awake, and Other Poems; The Way Things Are, and Other Poems;* and *The Malibu, and Other Poems.*

Myra Cohn Livingston was born on August 17, 1926, in Omaha, Nebraska. She loved books

LIVINGSTON HAD A COLLECTION OF MORE THAN **10,000** BOOKS
OF POETRY. SHE ALSO COLLECTED BOOKMARKS.

and reading when she was young. She started to write poems and stories as soon as she knew how to read. Myra's mother always encouraged her to write. She told Myra to write about things that she knew about. Myra remembered her mother's advice when she became a writer.

When she was eleven years old, Myra and her family moved to California. That same year, she began to play the French horn. She loved music, art, sculpture, and writing. She spent many hours practicing her French horn. She also joined a youth symphony and played in the group for five years.

> *"When you write a poem, either tell me something I have never heard before or tell me in a new way something I have heard before."*

Myra devoted a lot of time to writing as well. She wrote stories for the school newspaper. She also wrote poetry and plays. When she finished high school, Myra was not sure what she wanted to study in college. She loved writing and playing music. Her decision was made when she enrolled in Sarah Lawrence College in New York. The college did not have an orchestra, so she focused on her writing.

Myra Cohn Livingston wrote her first book of poetry when she was a college student. It was not published until twelve years later. The book, *Whispers, and Other Poems,* was her first book for children. It was

---

THE CHILDREN'S LITERATURE COUNCIL OF SOUTHERN CALIFORNIA CREATED THE MYRA COHN LIVINGSTON AWARD FOR POETRY IN 1999.

POET
Myra Cohn Livingston

A

CIRCLE
OF
SEASONS

Leonard Everett Fisher
PAINTER

A Selected Bibliography of Livingston's Work

Cricket Never Does: A Collection of Haiku and Tanka (1997)

B Is for Baby: An Alphabet of Verses (1996)

Call Down the Moon: Poems of Music (Selections, 1995)

Animal, Vegetable, Mineral: Poems about Small Things (Selections, 1994)

I Never Told and Other Poems (1992)

Let Freedom Ring: A Ballad of Martin Luther King, Jr. (1992)

Light & Shadow (1992)

Poem-Making: Ways to Begin Writing Poetry (1991)

Birthday Poems (1989)

Up in the Air (1989)

Earth Songs (1986)

A Circle of Seasons (1982)

The Way Things Are, and Other Poems (1974)

The Malibu, and Other Poems (1972)

Wide Awake, and Other Poems (1959)

Whispers, and Other Poems (1958)

published in 1958. She also had other poems published when she was a student.

When she finished college, Livingston returned to California. She worked for several newspapers and wrote book reviews.

She met her husband while visiting Dallas, Texas. After she was married, she lived in Dallas for about thirteen years. Livingston began teaching creative writing there. She taught classes for young people at the public library. She continued to teach creative writing after she and her family moved back to California.

Livingston's poetry is simple and easy to understand. Many of her poems deal with problems that children face. She won lots of awards for her own poetry and for anthologies of other writers' poetry she edited.

Livingston died on August 23, 1996, in Los Angeles, California. She was seventy years old.

> *"I believe the most important contribution I can make is to guide the young to become aware of their sensitivities and individuality and find a form in which to communicate these strengths to others."*

WHERE TO FIND OUT MORE ABOUT MYRA COHN LIVINGSTON

BOOKS

McElmeel, Sharron L. *100 Most Popular Children's Authors: Biographical Sketches and Bibliographies.* Englewood, Colo.: Libraries Unlimited, 1999.

Something about the Author. Autobiography Series. Vol. 1. Detroit: Gale Research, 1986.

Sutherland, Zena. *Children and Books.* New York: Addison Wesley Longman, 1997.

WEB SITE

CHILDREN'S LITERATURE COUNCIL
http://www.childrensliteraturecouncil.org/myra_cohn_livingston_award.htm
For information about Myra Cohn Livingston

EVEN AFTER BECOMING A WRITER, LIVINGSTON CONTINUED TO PLAY THE FRENCH HORN. SHE PERFORMED WITH PROFESSIONAL MUSICIANS SEVERAL TIMES THROUGHOUT HER LIFE.

Megan Lloyd

Born: November 5, 1958

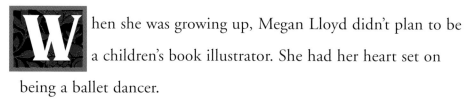

When she was growing up, Megan Lloyd didn't plan to be a children's book illustrator. She had her heart set on being a ballet dancer.

Megan took lessons throughout her childhood, and she—along with everyone else in her family—was sure she would become a profes-

sional ballerina. There was just one problem. When she was a teenager, Megan was only five feet, one inch tall. That was much too short to dance professionally. Megan was disappointed, but she soon found a new way to express herself. She became an artist.

Megan Lloyd was born on November 5, 1958, in Harrisburg,

LLOYD ENJOYS RESTORING ANTIQUE FURNITURE.

Pennsylvania. Her father and mother were both teachers. The family also included Megan's older sister, as well as a dog and a cat. The family was close and active, and they enjoyed sharing activities such as horseback riding.

Megan was fifteen years old when she realized that she would never be a professional ballet dancer. So she focused her creative energies on the visual arts instead. Luckily, her high school had an excellent art department. Megan's teachers encouraged and supported her as she explored painting and other art forms.

> *"Each book presents a new puzzle to solve."*

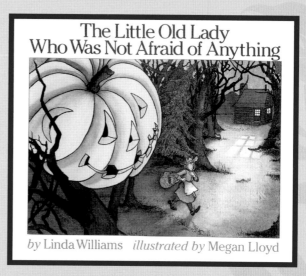

The Little Old Lady Who Was Not Afraid of Anything
by Linda Williams   *illustrated by* Megan Lloyd

A Selected Bibliography of Lloyd's Work

Mixed-up Rooster (2006)
Earthquakes (2005)
Fancy That! (2003)
Thanksgiving at the Tappletons' (2003)
Horse in the Pigpen (2002)
Heeey, Ma! (2002)
Pioneer Church (1999)
Chirping Crickets (1998)
Falcons Nest on Skyscrapers (1996)
Too Many Pumpkins (1996)
Dance with Me (1995)
The Perfectly Orderly House (1994)
The Gingerbread Doll (1993)
The Gingerbread Man (1993)
Lobster Boat (1993)
The Christmas Tree Ride (1992)
Look Out for Turtles! (1992)
Baba Yaga: A Russian Folktale (1991)
Cactus Hotel (1991)
Super Cluck (1991)
How We Learned the Earth Is Round (1990)
That Sky, That Rain (1990)
The Little Old Lady Who Was Not Afraid of Anything (1988)
More Surprises (1987)
The Atlantic Free Balloon Race (1986)
Farmer Mack Measures His Pig (1986)
All Those Mothers at the Manger (1985)
Surprises (1984)
Chicken Tricks (Text and illustrations, 1983)

Even though she loved painting, Megan decided she wanted to go to Harvard Law School and become a lawyer. To prepare for Harvard, she signed up for Pennsylvania State University's pre-law

> *"Many of the people, places, and animals around me wind up in my pictures. I have never been able to 'make up' pictures. I need to see what I want to draw."*

program after she graduated from high school in 1976. However, she was miserable studying law, and she missed her artistic work. She was totally confused about what she wanted to do with her life.

Megan Lloyd's mother came to the rescue. She suggested that Lloyd illustrate picture books, and she showed her daughter a book called *Circus,* by Brian Wildsmith. Lloyd was fascinated by the illustrations in the book and decided to give illustrating a try.

Lloyd went to New York City to study illustration at the Parsons

> *"The more I learn about illustrating books, the more I discover all that I don't know!"*

School of Design. After she graduated in 1981, she got a job in publishing. She worked for about a year as an art director's assistant at Harper Junior Books, where she learned about making picture books.

LLOYD IS TRAINING HER DOGS TO HERD SHEEP AND WORK AS SLED DOGS.

In 1983, Harper published Lloyd's first book, *Chicken Tricks.* Lloyd has not written any other children's books since then, but she has illustrated more than thirty books by other writers.

Lloyd lives with her husband, Thomas Thompson, and two dogs on a farm in Pennsylvania. She continues to be a popular illustrator of everything from nonfiction to folktales to poetry.

❧

WHERE TO FIND OUT MORE ABOUT MEGAN LLOYD

BOOKS

Rockman, Connie C., ed. *Eighth Book of Junior Authors and Illustrators.* New York: H. W. Wilson Company, 2000.

Something about the Author. Vol. 77. Detroit: Gale Research, 1994.

WEB SITE

MEGAN LLOYD HOME PAGE
www.meganlloyd.com
To read a short biography of Megan Lloyd and to see a gallery of her books

---

LLOYD HAS TRAVELED ALL OVER THE UNITED STATES
TO RESEARCH HER NONFICTION BOOKS.

Arnold Lobel

Born: May 22, 1933
Died: December 4, 1987

rnold Lobel wanted to use his books for children to teach important lessons. Some of his most famous books are about Frog and Toad. He used these two funny characters to teach children about how to be a good friend.

Lobel has written and illustrated many other books for children. His best-known books include *A Holiday for Mister Muster*, *Frog and Toad All Year*, *Days with Frog and Toad*, and *Ming Lo Moves the Mountain*.

Arnold Lobel was born on May 22, 1933, in Los Angeles, California. Shortly after he was born, Arnold and his family moved to Schenectady, New York.

MUCH OF LOBEL'S INSPIRATION FOR HIS BOOKS CAME FROM REMEMBERING HIS OWN CHILDHOOD AND FROM OBSERVING THE CARTOONS HIS OWN CHILDREN LIKED TO WATCH.

When he was in kindergarten, first, and second grades, Arnold was sick a lot. He missed many days of school because he was in the hospital or at home. It was hard for him to make friends because he was not in school very much.

By the time Arnold was in third grade, he was healthier. He used his inter-

> *"Somehow in the writing of the manuscript for* Frog and Toad *I was, for the first time, able to write about myself. Frog and Toad are really two aspects of myself."*

est in drawing and storytelling to make friends. He had drawn many pictures on the days that he was not in school. When he returned to school, he shared his pictures with his new friends. His friends loved to hear Arnold's stories, too.

When he entered high school, Arnold decided that he wanted to become an artist. He studied the illustrations of many artists. He wanted to learn how other artists did their work.

When he graduated from high school, he attended art school in Brooklyn, New York. Lobel met his wife at the school. She also became an author and illustrator of children's books.

While he attended art school, Lobel lived in an apartment near the zoo. He often went to the zoo to draw pictures of the animals.

LOBEL NEVER LIKED TO USE THE SAME TECHNIQUE TO ILLUSTRATE DIFFERENT BOOKS. INSTEAD, HE PREFERRED TO VARY HIS STYLE DEPENDING ON THE TONE OF THE MANUSCRIPT.

A Selected Bibliography of Lobel's Work

The Arnold Lobel Book of Mother Goose
(Selections and illustrations, 1997)

The Just Right Mother Goose (Illustrations only, 1996)

Whiskers & Rhymes (1985)

The Rose in My Garden (1984)

The Book of Pigericks: Pig Limericks (1983)

Ming Lo Moves the Mountain (1982)

On Market Street (1981)

Fables (1980)

Days with Frog and Toad (1979)

Grasshopper on the Road (1978)

Frog and Toad All Year (1976)

Mouse Tales (1972)

Frog and Toad Together (1972)

Hildilid's Night (Illustrations only, 1971)

Frog and Toad Are Friends (1970)

A Holiday for Mister Muster (1963)

A Zoo for Mister Muster (1962)

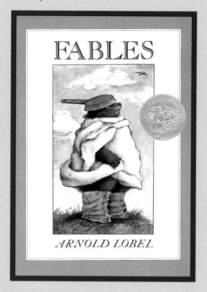

Lobel's Major Literary Awards

1984 Boston Globe-Horn Book Picture Book Honor Book
  The Rose in My Garden

1982 Caldecott Honor Book
1981 Boston Globe-Horn Book Picture Book Honor Book
  On Market Street

1981 Caldecott Medal
  Fables

1973 Newbery Honor Book
  Frog and Toad Together

1972 Caldecott Honor Book
  Hildilid's Night

1971 Caldecott Honor Book
  Frog and Toad Are Friends

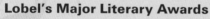

"I cannot think of any work that could be more agreeable and fun than making books for children."

His many trips to the zoo inspired him to write and illustrate his first children's book. The book, *A Zoo for Mister Muster,* was published in 1962.

Lobel used different styles of illustrations in his books. Some of his books are illustrated with pencil drawings. In other books, he used many colors for the pictures. In writing his stories, he always included humor.

Lobel wrote and illustrated more than thirty-five books for children. He also illustrated more than sixty-five books written by other authors.

Arnold Lobel died of a heart attack on December 4, 1987, in New York. He was fifty-four years old.

❧

WHERE TO FIND OUT MORE ABOUT ARNOLD LOBEL

BOOKS

Kovacs, Deborah, and James Preller. *Meet the Authors and Illustrators: 60 Creators of Favorite Children's Books Talk About Their Work.* Vol. 1. New York: Scholastic, 1991.

McElmeel, Sharron L. *100 Most Popular Picture Book Authors and Illustrators: Biographical Sketches and Bibliographies.* Englewood, Colo.: Libraries Unlimited, 2000.

Rockman, Connie C., ed. *The Ninth Book of Junior Authors and Illustrators.* New York: H. W. Wilson Company, 2004.

Silvey, Anita, ed. *The Essential Guide to Children's Books and Their Creators.* Boston: Houghton Mifflin Company, 2002.

Sutherland, Zena. *Children and Books.* New York: Addison Wesley Longman, 1997.

WEB SITES

EDUCATIONAL PAPERBACK ASSOCIATION
http://edupaperback.org/showauth.cfm?authid=242
To read an autobiographical sketch of and a booklist for Arnold Lobel

MEET THE AUTHOR
http://www.carolhurst.com/authors/alobel.html
For biographical information about Arnold Lobel

———

BOOK REVIEWERS ADMIRED LOBEL'S FABLES, SAYING THAT THE CHARACTERS TEACH IMPORTANT LESSONS BUT IN A LIGHTHEARTED WAY.

Thomas Locker

Born: June 26, 1937

Thomas Locker's two favorite things in the world are art and nature. Throughout his career as a painter and children's book illustrator, he has been able to combine these two loves to create beauty in several different forms.

Thomas Locker was born on June 26, 1937, in New

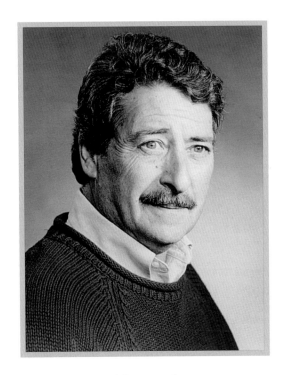

York City. His father was a political lobbyist, and his mother was a book dealer. Although Thomas lived in the city, he made many visits to the country, too. He soon learned to love the beauty of the country-side, which was so different from his city home.

LOCKER DISCOVERED ILLUSTRATED CHILDREN'S BOOKS
WHILE READING TO HIS FIVE SONS.

Locker graduated from the University of Chicago in 1960. He went on to receive a master of fine arts degree from American University in Washington, D.C.

Although Locker loved to paint, his first job was as a teacher. From 1963 to 1973, he was a professor of art at several colleges in the Midwest. Locker continued to paint during his years as a college professor.

By 1973, Thomas Locker had shown his paintings at art galleries all around the United States. That year, Locker made a big decision: He left teaching and became a full-time artist.

During the 1960s and 1970s, Locker was also busy

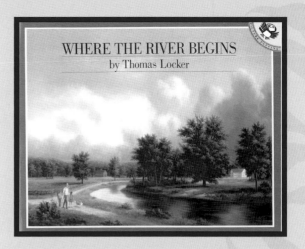

WHERE THE RIVER BEGINS
by Thomas Locker

A Selected Bibliography of Locker's Work

Hudson: A Story of a River (2004)
John Muir, America's Naturalist (2003)
Mountain Dance (2001)
Cloud Dance (2000)
In Blue Mountains: An Artist's Return to America's First Wilderness (2000)
Grandfather's Christmas Tree (Illustrations only, 1999)
Water Dance (1997)
Between Earth & Sky: Legends of Native American Sacred Places (Illustrations only, 1996)
The Earth Under Sky Bear's Feet: Native American Poems of the Land (Illustrations only, 1995)
Sky Tree: Seeing Science through Art (1995)
Anna and the Bagpiper (1994)
The First Thanksgiving (Illustrations only, 1993)
Calico and Tin Horns (Illustrations only, 1992)
Thirteen Moons on Turtle's Back: A Native American Year of Moons (Illustrations only, 1992)
Catskill Eagle (Illustrations only, 1991)
The Land of Gray Wolf (1991)
Snow toward Evening: A Year in River Valley: Nature Poems (Illustrations only, 1990)
The Young Artist (1989)
Family Farm (1988)
Washington Irving's Rip Van Winkle (1988)
The Boy Who Held Back the Sea (Illustrations only, 1987)
The Ugly Duckling (Illustrations only, 1987)
Sailing with the Wind (1986)
The Mare on the Hill (1985)
Miranda's Smile (1984)
Where the River Begins (1984)

> "I see my books as a kind of bridge between generations and a way to bring fine art to the young mind."

raising a family. He married Marea Panares Teske in 1964. The couple had a son, Anthony, before they divorced in 1971.

Then Locker married Maria Adelman. They had four more sons—Aaron, Josh, Jonathan, and Gregory.

During the 1970s and early 1980s, Locker had a successful career as a landscape painter. Then he decided to try his hand at children's books.

Locker's first book was *Where the River Begins.* It was published in 1984. Like many of his later books, this book focuses on young characters exploring the natural world. The painterly illustration is detailed and sophisticated. Locker has also illustrated many books by other authors.

Many of Locker's books, such as *Water Dance, Cloud Dance,* and *Mountain Dance,* describe natural events and places, such as rainstorms or the seashore. Locker also enjoys writing about artists. Creating artwork is a major theme in *Miranda's Smile* and *The Young Artist.*

> "I gave [illustrating children's books] a try as a lark and now I devote most of my time to books."

LOCKER'S PAINTINGS HAVE BEEN SHOWN IN LONDON, ENGLAND, AS WELL AS IN LOS ANGELES, NEW YORK, AND OTHER MAJOR U.S. CITIES.

Today, Locker lives in Stuyvesant, New York. He continues to paint and create new works to delight both children and adults. "I rejoice in the expressive potential of joining words with images and painting in narrative order," Locker explains.

❧

WHERE TO FIND OUT MORE ABOUT THOMAS LOCKER

BOOKS

Holtze, Sally Holmes, ed. *Sixth Book of Junior Authors & Illustrators.*
New York: H. W. Wilson Company, 1989.

Locker, Thomas. *The Man Who Paints Nature.*
Katonah, N.Y.: Richard C. Owen, 1999.

Sutherland, Zena, and May Hill Arbuthnot, eds. *Children and Books.*
7th ed. New York: Addison Wesley Longman, 1986.

WEB SITES

IN BLUE MOUNTAINS: OIL PAINTINGS BY THOMAS LOCKER
http://www.thomaslocker.com/pages/biography.html
To read a biographical sketch of Thomas Locker and view some of his art

THOMAS LOCKER HOME PAGE
http://www.lib.uconn.edu/Exhibits/locker/ThomasLocker.htm
To see some of Thomas Locker's paintings

LOCKER HAS WON MANY AWARDS, INCLUDING THE *NEW YORK TIMES* AWARD FOR ILLUSTRATION, THE CHRISTOPHER AWARD, AND THE JOHN BURROUGHS AWARD.

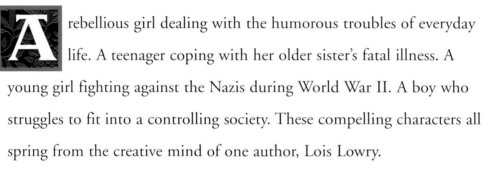

Lois Lowry

Born: March 20, 1937

A rebellious girl dealing with the humorous troubles of everyday life. A teenager coping with her older sister's fatal illness. A young girl fighting against the Nazis during World War II. A boy who struggles to fit into a controlling society. These compelling characters all spring from the creative mind of one author, Lois Lowry.

Lois Lowry was born on March 20, 1937, in Honolulu, Hawaii. Her maiden name is Lois Hammersberg. Her father was an army dentist. During World War II (1939–1945), her father served with the U.S. Army while Lois, her mother, her older sister, and her younger brother lived with Lois's grandparents in Pennsylvania. Lois missed her father terribly during those years. She was thrilled when the family was finally reunited after the war.

LOWRY SPENT PART OF HER CHILDHOOD IN TOKYO, JAPAN, WHILE HER FATHER WAS STATIONED THERE WITH THE ARMY.

Lois always loved books. She learned to read at the age of three. When she started school, Lois preferred to sit alone with a book rather than join her classmates in playing games.

Lois was only sixteen when she graduated from high school. She was determined to be a writer, and she enrolled at Brown University in Rhode Island in 1954. However, she dropped out of school after only two years when she married a naval officer named Donald Grey Lowry. The couple had four children before they divorced in 1977.

Although Lowry enjoyed being a wife and mother, she was unhappy about having to drop out of school to raise a family. Finally, in 1972, Lowry was able to complete her education. She received a degree from the University of Southern Maine. While she was in school, she and her children did their homework together at the kitchen table.

During the 1970s, Lowry's short stories began appearing in magazines. She also wrote several literature textbooks. Then, in 1977, Lowry published her first novel, *A Summer to Die.* This book tells the story of a thirteen-year-old girl who must face the death of her older sister and rival. The novel received excellent reviews, and Lowry's career as a children's book author was born.

"The most important things to me in my own life, as well as in my books, are human relationships of all kinds."

LOWRY SKIPPED TWO GRADES IN SCHOOL AND WAS USUALLY THE YOUNGEST AND SMALLEST STUDENT IN HER CLASS.

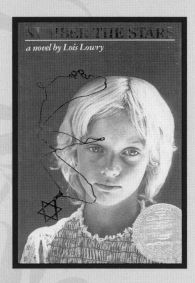

A Selected Bibliography of Lowry's Work

Gossamer (2006)
Messenger (2004)
Silent Boy (2003)
Gooney Bird Greene (2002)
Gathering Blue (2000)
Zooman Sam (1999)
Looking Back: A Book of Memories (1998)
See You Around, Sam (1996)
Anastasia, Absolutely (1995)
The Giver (1993)
Attaboy, Sam! (1992)
Number the Stars (1989)
Anastasia's Chosen Career (1987)
Rabble Starkey (1986)
Anastasia, Ask Your Analyst (1984)
The One Hundredth Thing about Caroline (1983)
Anastasia Again! (1981)
Autumn Street (1980)
Anastasia Krupnik (1979)
Find a Stranger, Say Goodbye (1978)
A Summer to Die (1977)

Lowry's Major Literary Awards

1994 Newbery Medal
1993 Boston Globe-Horn Book Fiction Honor Book
   The Giver
1990 Newbery Medal
   Number the Stars
1987 Boston Globe-Horn Book Fiction Award
   Rabble Starkey

Lowry has written many kinds of books during her long career. Some of her books, such as *Rabble Starkey,* are serious, but she wrote humorous stories as well. Perhaps Lowry's most popular works are the books about Anastasia Krupnik. These stories focus on a spunky preteen girl who faces everyday problems such as troublesome parents, the embarrassments of gym class, and the arrival of a baby brother.

"I think, in general, anybody who wants to write anything should a, read a lot and b, write a lot, and quit worrying about who's going to buy it."

During the 1990s, Lowry became one of the most respected authors for young readers. In 1990, her book *Number the Stars* won the prestigious Newbery Medal as the best children's novel of the year. *Number the Stars* looks at life under the Nazis from a child's point of view. In 1994, Lowry won her second Newbery Medal for *The Giver,* a science fiction novel about a futuristic society.

Today, Lowry lives in New England. She enjoys her family—which now includes several grandchildren—and continues to write funny, tragic, haunting, and always compelling stories about young people.

❧

WHERE TO FIND OUT MORE ABOUT LOIS LOWRY

BOOKS

Hill, Christine M. *Ten Terrific Authors for Teens.*
Berkeley Heights, N.J.: Enslow Publishers, 2000.

Lowry, Lois. *Looking Back: A Book of Memories.*
Boston: Houghton Mifflin, 1998.

McElmeel, Sharron L. *100 Most Popular Children's Authors: Biographical Sketches and Bibliographies.* Englewood, Colo.: Libraries Unlimited, 1999.

WEB SITES

THE INTERNET PUBLIC LIBRARY
http://www.ipl.org/div/kidspace/askauthor/Lowry.html
To read an autobiographical sketch of Lois Lowry and the transcript of an interview

LOIS LOWRY HOME PAGE
http://www.loislowry.com/
To read a biography and other information about Lois Lowry

LOWRY TOOK THE PHOTOGRAPH THAT APPEARS ON THE COVER OF *THE GIVER.*

David Macaulay

Born: December 2, 1946

David Macaulay uses words and pictures to show and tell how the everyday objects around us work. His books explore how buildings are built and how wheels go around. Macaulay's drawings for each book are as entertaining as they are informative. If readers look at the drawings closely, they will find small stories unfolding in each scene. Macaulay hopes these images will stay with his readers.

David Macaulay was born on December 2, 1946, in Burton-on-Trent, England. His father worked on machines for the textile industry. As a boy, David watched his father working on do-it-yourself projects around the house. He, too, became interested in the inner workings of things. He began building cardboard models of

SEVERAL OF MACAULAY'S BOOKS HAVE BEEN TURNED INTO TELEVISION SERIES.

skyscrapers, complete with elevators that he could raise and lower with a string.

Macaulay also fondly remembers the long walk through woods to his school. He liked to daydream and let his imagination roam free during the walk.

David and his family moved to the United States when he was eleven. In high school, he discovered that his talent for drawing could make him popular. He won friends by making drawings of the Beatles and other stars.

After graduation from high school, David Macaulay attended the Rhode Island School of Design, where he studied architecture. However,

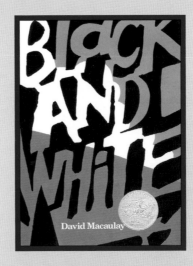

A Selected Bibliography of Macaulay's Work

Mosque (2003)
Angelo's Work (2002)
Building Big (2000)
Building the Book Cathedral (1999)
The New Way Things Work (1998)
Why the Chicken Crossed the Road (1997)
Black and White (1990)
The Way Things Work (1988)
Baaa (1985)
Unbuilding (1980)
Motel of the Mysteries (1979)
Great Moments in Architecture (1978)
Castle (1977)
Underground (1976)
Pyramid (1975)
City: A Story of Roman Planning and Construction (1974)
Cathedral: The Story of Its Construction (1973)

Macaulay's Major Literary Awards

1991 Caldecott Medal
   Black and White
1989 Boston Globe–Horn Book Nonfiction Honor Book
   The Way Things Work
1978 Boston Globe–Horn Book Nonfiction Honor Book
1978 Caldecott Honor Book
   Castle
1976 Boston Globe–Horn Book Nonfiction Honor Book
   Pyramid
1974 Caldecott Honor Book
   Cathedral: The Story of Its Construction

> "*I want to communicate. . . .*
> *For me the point is to leave*
> *a picture in somebody's*
> *mind—not necessarily a*
> *sentence or a paragraph.*"

he never worked as an architect. Instead, he worked at a number of jobs, including teaching art to junior-high students.

His first book began as a story about a beauty pageant for gargoyles—the scary mythological creatures carved on the walls of cathedrals. Editors at one publishing company liked his drawings for the book, but they didn't like the beauty pageant story. Instead, Macaulay changed the book so that it told how a cathedral was built. *Cathedral: The Story of Its Construction* was published in 1973. It won several awards, including one as the best illustrated children's book of the year.

Over the next seven years, Macaulay produced a different book each year. His second book was *City: A Story of Roman Planning and Construction.* It took readers on a tour of an ancient Roman city. *Pyramid* explored the huge monuments to ancient Egyptian pharaohs. *Castle* revealed the inner workings of a medieval European fortress.

> "*We create all these things and*
> *then we think of ourselves as too*
> *stupid to understand them. . . .*
> *I hope [my work] says to readers,*
> '*You can figure it out.*'"

SOME OF MACAULAY'S DRAWINGS ARE IN THE COLLECTIONS OF ART MUSEUMS, INCLUDING THE COOPER HEWITT MUSEUM AND THE TOLEDO MUSEUM OF ART.

In 1988, Macaulay published *The Way Things Work*. His detailed drawings and clear writing helped readers understand even the most complicated gadgets. The book shows what makes cars run, how nail clippers clip, and the scientific principle behind a seesaw.

Despite his complex subjects, Macaulay makes his books entertaining and humorous. He lives with his family in Providence, Rhode Island.

❧

WHERE TO FIND OUT MORE ABOUT DAVID MACAULAY

BOOKS

McElmeel, Sharron L. *100 Most Popular Picture Book Authors and Illustrators: Biographical Sketches and Bibliographies.* Englewood, Colo.: Libraries Unlimited, 2000.

Norby, Shirley, and Gregory Ryan. *Famous Illustrators of Children's Literature.* Minneapolis: T. S. Denison, 1992.

Silvey, Anita, ed. *The Essential Guide to Children's Books and Their Creators.* Boston: Houghton Mifflin Company, 2002.

Something about the Author. Vol. 46. Detroit: Gale Research, 1987.

WEB SITES

BUILDING BIG: LIVE CHAT WITH DAVID MACAULAY
http://www.pbs.org/wgbh/buildingbig/chat.html
To read a live chat transcript with Macaulay

HOUGHTON MIFFLIN BOOKS
http://www.houghtonmifflinbooks.com/features/davidmacaulay/bio.shtml
To read a biographical sketch of David Macaulay, a booklist, and book reviews

---

MACAULAY CONSIDERS HIMSELF FIRST AND FOREMOST AN ILLUSTRATOR.

Patricia MacLachlan

Born: March 3, 1938

atricia MacLachlan is an award-winning author of picture books and novels for children. She is best known as the author of *Sarah, Plain and Tall.* MacLachlan's other books include *The Sick Day, The Facts and Fictions of Minna Pratt,* and *Arthur, for the Very First Time.*

Patricia MacLachlan was born on March 3, 1938, in Cheyenne, Wyoming. She was an only child and had a close relationship with her parents. Both of her parents were teachers. She read many books by herself and with her family. "We read them, discussed them, reread them and acted out the parts," MacLachlan remembers.

As a young girl, Patricia did not write stories, but she used her imagination to create fantasies about Mary, an imaginary friend of hers. MacLachlan notes that "Mary was real

ACTRESS GLENN CLOSE STARRED IN THE
TELEVISION PRODUCTION OF *SARAH, PLAIN AND TALL.*

enough for me to insist that my parents set a place for her at the table."
Her parents encouraged Patricia to use her imagination.

Patricia and her family moved to Minnesota for a few years before
she went on to college. She attended the University of Connecticut. After
she graduated, she taught English. She also got married and had three
children.

MacLachlan then began working at a social-service agency while she
was still raising her own children at home. At the agency, MacLachlan
worked with foster mothers. She wrote a
series of journal articles about adoption
and foster mothers. These are themes that
later became important in her writing for
children. "It was clear to me that much
of the focus of my writing was sharp-
ened by my involvement and concern for
families and children," MacLachlan says.

*"I feel it's crucial that kids who
aspire to write understand that I
have to rewrite and revise as they
do. Ours is such a perfectionist
society—I see too many kids who
believe that if they don't get it right
the first time, they aren't writers."*

As her children grew older and
entered school, MacLachlan felt she needed to do something else. "It
dawned on me that what I really wanted to do was to write," she recalls.
MacLachlan began her career as a children's author by writing picture
books. Before she wrote her first book, MacLachlan read hundreds of

MACLACHLAN DIDN'T BEGIN HER
WRITING CAREER UNTIL SHE WAS THIRTY-FIVE YEARS OLD.

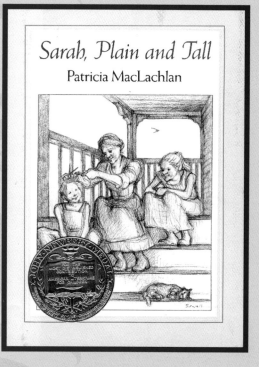

Sarah, Plain and Tall
Patricia MacLachlan

A Selected Bibliography of MacLachlan's Work

Grandfather's Dance (2006)

Who Loves Me? (2005)

More Perfect Than the Moon (2004)

Painting the Wind (2003)

Caleb's Story (2001)

All the Places to Love (1994)

Skylark (1994)

Baby (1993)

Journey (1991)

The Facts and Fictions of Minna Pratt (1988)

Sarah, Plain and Tall (1985)

Unclaimed Treasures (1984)

Cassie Binegar (1982)

Tomorrow's Wizard (1982)

Arthur, for the Very First Time (1980)

The Sick Day (1979)

MacLachlan's Major Literary Awards

1986 Newbery Medal
1986 Scott O'Dell Award
  Sarah, Plain and Tall

1984 Boston Globe-Horn Book Nonfiction Honor Book
  Unclaimed Treasures

children's books. Her first book, *The Sick Day,* was published in 1979.

After writing several picture books, MacLachlan was encouraged by her editor to write novels for young people. Her first novel, *Arthur, for the Very First Time,* was published in 1980. She found that picture books were more difficult to write than a novel. "A good picture book is much like a poem," MacLachlan notes.

In her books, MacLachlan writes about things that happen in everyday life. "My books derive chiefly from my family life, both as a child with my own parents as well as with my husband and kids," MacLachlan says. She believes that young people can relate better to things that could and do happen to them.

Along with writing, MacLachlan teaches a course on children's literature at Smith College. She gives lectures on writing and visits schools to talk about her books with children. She also gives writing workshops for children. MacLachlan lives with her family in Massachusetts, where she continues to write.

> *"Writing for children is special because I think children read with a great true belief in what they're reading."*

❧

WHERE TO FIND OUT MORE ABOUT PATRICIA MACLACHLAN

BOOKS

McElmeel, Sharron L. *100 Most Popular Children's Authors: Biographical Sketches and Bibliographies.* Englewood, Colo.: Libraries Unlimited, 1999.

Silvey, Anita, ed. *The Essential Guide to Children's Books and Their Creators.* Boston: Houghton Mifflin Company, 2002.

WEB SITES

EDUCATIONAL PAPERBACK ASSOCIATION
http://edupaperback.org/showauth.cfm?authid=34
To read a biographical sketch of and a booklist for Patricia MacLachlan

HARPERCHILDRENS.COM: PATRICIA MACLACHLAN
http://www.harperchildrens.com/catalog/author_xml.asp?authorid=12425
To read an autobiography of Patricia MacLachlan and to see the covers of many of her books

———

THE CHARACTERS AUNT ELDA AND UNCLE WRISBY, WHO APPEAR IN THE BOOK *ARTHUR, FOR THE VERY FIRST TIME,* ARE MODELED AFTER MACLACHLAN'S MOTHER AND FATHER.

Margaret Mahy

Born: March 21, 1936

argaret Mahy's job as a librarian helped her to be a better writer. "Being a librarian certainly helped me even more with my writing because it made me even more of a reader," Mahy says. After working as a librarian, Mahy went on to become a children's author. Her most popular books include *The Haunting; The Changeover: A Supernatural Romance; The Tricksters;* and *Memory.*

Margaret Mahy was born on March 21, 1936, in Whakatane, New Zealand. She is the oldest of five children. Her father would tell the children stories and read to them. Her father's stories of adventure inspired Margaret to become a writer.

Margaret had one of her stories published in a newspaper when she was eight years old. She also entered many of her stories in writing contests.

MARGARET MAHY HAS A VERY OLD CAT NAMED ORSINO.
THE CAT SLEEPS ON HER FAX MACHINE BECAUSE IT IS ALWAYS WARM!

Margaret had a happy childhood. Many of her family's relatives lived in the same town. She loved to spend time with her family, who were very important to her. When she became a writer, she often wrote about family life.

In high school, Margaret was a very good student. She was also a very good swimmer. When she finished high school, she worked as a nurse's aide for six months. She then went on to college.

Mahy studied at college to become a librarian. She found a job as a librarian when she finished college. She worked at many different libraries in New Zealand and England before becoming a full-time writer in 1980.

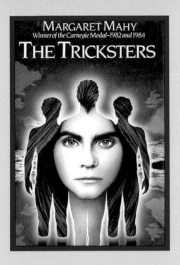

A Selected Bibliography of Mahy's Work

Down the Back of the Chair (2006)
Alchemy (2003)
Dashing Dog (2002)
Down the Dragon's Tongue (2000)
Twenty-Four Hours (2000)
Simply Delicious! (1999)
Don't Read This! And Other Tales of the Unnatural (1998)
Busy Day for a Good Grandmother (1995)
My Mysterious World (1995)
The Catalogue of the Universe (1994)
Dangerous Spaces (1991)
The Door in the Air and Other Stories (1991)
The Seven Chinese Brothers (1990)
Memory (1988)
The Tricksters (1986)
Aliens in the Family (1985)
The Haunting (1982)
The Boy Who Was Followed Home (1975)
Ultra-Violet Catastrophe (1975)
The Changeover: A Supernatural Romance (1974)
A Lion in the Meadow (1969)

Mahy's Major Literary Awards

2006 Hans Christian Andersen Medal for Authors

1988 Boston Globe–Horn Book Fiction Honor Book
    Memory

1985 Boston Globe–Horn Book Fiction Honor Book
1984 Carnegie Medal
    The Changeover: A Supernatural Romance

1982 Carnegie Medal
    The Haunting

While she was working as a librarian, Mahy wrote poems and stories. She tried to get her writing published by companies in New Zealand. She had a few stories published there in the early 1960s.

Mahy became more successful when her first book was published in the United States. The book, *A Lion in the Meadow,* was published in 1969. Mahy went on to have many more of her picture books, novels, nonfiction books, and book series published throughout the world.

Mahy writes for many different age groups of children. "I don't think I prefer writing for one age group above another," Mahy notes. "I am just as pleased with a story which I feel works well for very small children as I am with a story for young adults." In her writing, Mahy often uses humor. She also writes about real issues that young people may experience.

> *". . . I was obsessed not only with writing the stories down, but with trying to get them glorified by print. I will never forget the astonishment that flooded me when, at age eight, I opened a local newspaper to the children's column and saw a story of mine in print for the first time."*

Mahy grew up listening to stories set in England. She eventually began to write stories that take place in New Zealand. All of her young adult books take place in New Zealand.

———

MAHY'S STORIES HAVE BEEN TRANSLATED INTO FIFTEEN LANGUAGES.

Mahy continues to write for children and young people , and she is a great encouragement to other New Zealand writers. She lives with her family and a large assortment of pets in Governor's Bay, New Zealand.

> *"I have told children all the truth I know from personal experience."*

❧

WHERE TO FIND OUT MORE ABOUT MARGARET MAHY

BOOKS

Kovacs, Deborah, and James Preller. *Meet the Authors and Illustrators: 60 Creators of Favorite Children's Books Talk About Their Work.* Vol. 1. New York: Scholastic, 1991.

Mahy, Margaret. *My Mysterious World.*
Katonah, N.Y.: R.C. Owen, 1995.

Rockman, Connie C., ed. *The Ninth Book of Junior Authors and Illustrators.*
New York: H. W. Wilson Company, 2004.

Silvey, Anita, ed. *The Essential Guide to Children's Books and Their Creators.*
Boston: Houghton Mifflin Company, 2002.

WEB SITES

CHRISTCHURCH CITY LIBRARIES
http://library.christchurch.org.nz/Childrens/MargaretMahy/about.asp
To read a biographical sketch of Margaret Mahy, a booklist, and a selection of awards

NEW ZEALAND WRITERS: MARGARET MAHY
http://www.bookcouncil.org/nz/writers/mahym.html
For biographical information about Mahy, along with her answers to readers' questions about her life and work

———

MAHY WROTE MANY SCRIPTS FOR NEW ZEALAND TELEVISION, INCLUDING *THE MARGARET MAHY STORY BOOK THEATRE, CUCKOOLAND,* AND *A LAND CALLED HAPPY.*

James Marshall

Born: October 10, 1942
Died: October 13, 1992

James Marshall is remembered for being a talented artist. He was dedicated to the business of children's books, and he had a passion for his work. *George and Martha* was the first of more than thirty-five books written and illustrated by Marshall.

James Marshall was born on October 10, 1942, in San Antonio, Texas. He grew up on a farm sixteen miles outside of the city. James's father had a dance band, and his mother sang in the church choir. Coming from this musical family, James planned to become a violist. He even won a scholarship to attend the New England Conservatory of Music. But he injured his hand during an airplane trip and had to change his plans.

SUBSTITUTE TEACHER VIOLA SWAMP IN THE MISS NELSON BOOKS IS BASED ON MARSHALL'S SECOND-GRADE TEACHER, WHO HAS SEEN THE BOOKS AND THINKS THEY'RE FUNNY.

Marshall attended Trinity University back home in Texas. His French teacher was Harry Allard. The two men later worked together on several series of books. Marshall finished college at Southern Connecticut State College, where he earned a degree in history and French. He got a job teaching Spanish and French at a high school in Boston—even though he had to learn Spanish as he went along.

While he was teaching, Marshall resumed his old hobby of drawing. (He had given it up back in second grade when a teacher laughed at him.) A friend intro- duced him to a book editor, and Marshall was given his first assign-

> *"People have very odd ideas of what a children's writer should be like. Children always expect me to look like a hippopota- mus and adults assume that by nature I have to be a little off the wall."*

ment. He got the job of illustrating *Plink, Plink, Plink* by Byrd Baylor, which was published in 1971.

Next, Marshall came up with a story of his own. *George and Martha*, published in 1972, is the tale of two hippos. It was the first of seven stories about these hippo friends. Years later, when all the George and Martha stories were collected in one volume, it was 340 pages long.

Marshall had several popular series of books in addition to the George and Martha books. The books in the Stupids series, several of

MARSHALL ONCE HAD A DREAM IN WHICH MARTHA COMPLAINED ABOUT HIS STORIES. SHE WANTED BETTER LINES—AND IF SHE DIDN'T GET THEM, SHE THREATENED TO GO TO ANOTHER ILLUSTRATOR'S HOUSE.

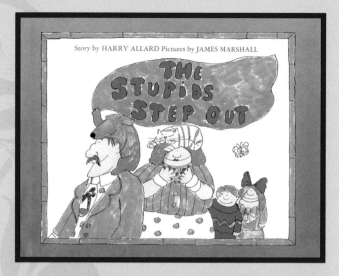

Story by HARRY ALLARD Pictures by JAMES MARSHALL

THE STUPIDS STEP OUT

A Selected Bibliography of Marshall's Work

James Marshall's Cinderella (Illustrations only, 2001)
Eugene (2000)
Swine Lake (1999)
The Owl and the Pussycat (Illustrations only, 1998)
George and Martha: The Complete Stories about Two Best Friends (1997)
Pocketful of Nonsense (1993)
The Cut-Ups Crack Up (1992)
Rats on the Roof and Other Stories (1991)
The Stupids Take Off (with Harry Allard, 1989)
Goldilocks and the Three Bears (1988)
Red Riding Hood (1987)
The Stupids Die (Illustrations only, 1981)
The Cut-Ups (1984)
Troll Country (1980)
Portly McSwine (1979)
Miss Nelson Is Missing! (with Harry Allard, 1977)
Mary Alice, Operator Number 9 (Illustrations only, 1975)
The Stupids Step Out (Illustrations only, 1974)
George and Martha (1972)
Plink, Plink, Plink (Illustrations only, 1971)

Marshall's Major Literary Awards

1999 Boston Globe–Horn Book Picture Book Honor Book
   The Owl and the Pussycat
1989 Caldecott Honor Book
   Goldilocks and the Three Bears

which he wrote with Allard, were about a family so foolish that (in one book) when the lights go out they think they've all died. The Cut-Ups books told the adventures of two wild boys, Joe and Spud, and their battle against the cranky school principal, Lamar J. Spurgle. There was also a series of books about a young fox, which Marshall wrote under the name Edward Marshall. For a while, Marshall pretended that Edward was a peculiar cousin of his from Texas. He also wrote adaptations of fairy tales and illustrated books by many other authors.

Marshall's style of drawing was extremely simple. His friend Maurice Sendak compared him with great illustrators such as

Randolph Caldecott and Jean de Brunhoff (who wrote and illustrated the Babar books). Sendak pointed to a picture in which Martha the hippo is planning a trick on George. "How did Marshall convey dementia, malice and get-evenness with two mere flicks of his pen for eyes?" he wondered.

> *"A book must have a good beginning and a strong middle, but without a knock-out ending, you're shot."*

Marshall was a funny, lively man who loved food and music and friendship. Sendak called him "a wicked angel" for his wit and warmth. He died on October 13, 1992, at the age of fifty.

ᕙ

WHERE TO FIND OUT MORE ABOUT JAMES MARSHALL

BOOKS
De Montreville, Doris, and Elizabeth D. Crawford, eds.
Fourth Book of Junior Authors & Illustrators. New York: H. W. Wilson Company, 1978.

Kovacs, Deborah, and James Preller. *Meet the Authors and Illustrators: 60 Creators of Favorite Children's Books Talk about Their Work.* Vol. 2. New York: Scholastic, 1993.

WEB SITES
CAROL HURST'S CHILDREN'S LITERATURE SITE
http://www.carolhurst.com/newsletters/42enewsletters.html
To read a biographical sketch of James Marshall and descriptions of some of his books

THE HORN BOOK
http://www.hbook.com/Exhibit/marshallbio.html
To read biographical information about James Marshall

WHILE MARSHALL WAS CREATING HIS FAMOUS HIPPOS,
EDWARD ALBEE'S PLAY *WHO'S AFRAID OF VIRGINIA WOOLF?* WAS ON TELEVISION.
THE PLAY IS ABOUT AN UNHAPPY COUPLE NAMED GEORGE AND MARTHA.

Ann M. Martin

Born: August 12, 1955

There are few children's authors who have written more books for young girls than Ann M. Martin. She is best known as the author of the Baby-Sitters Club series and the Baby-Sitters Little Sister series. There are nearly 125 million copies of books from these series in print.

Ann M. Martin was born on August 12, 1955, in Princeton, New Jersey. Ann's mother was a preschool teacher, and her father was an artist. "I grew up in a very imaginative family," Martin notes. She enjoyed writing and reading stories from the time she was very young. "Before I could write, I dictated stories to my mother," Martin remembers.

LEWIS CARROLL, ASTRID LINDGREN, AND ROALD DAHL ARE A FEW
OF THE AUTHORS MARTIN ENJOYED READING WHEN SHE WAS A CHILD.

When Martin enrolled at Smith College, she wanted to be a teacher. She graduated in 1977 and worked as an elementary school teacher in Connecticut for one year. She enjoyed teaching, but she decided she wanted to get a job with a children's publishing company.

Martin worked as an editor for two children's publishing companies. She also began writing children's books during that time. Her first book, *Bummer Summer,* was published in 1983. She wrote several other books and then decided to be a full-time writer in 1985. This is when she started the Baby-Sitters Club series.

Martin's editor came up with the idea for a series of

A Selected Bibliography of Martin's Work

On Christmas Eve (2006)
Here Today (2004)
A Corner of the Universe (2002)
Belle Teal (2001)
Snail Mail No More (2000)
Rachel Parker, Kindergarten Show-off (1992)
Eleven Kids, One Summer (1991)
Ma and Pa Dracula (1989)
Ten Kids, No Pets (1989)
Missing Since Monday (1986)
Me and Katie (the Pest) (1985)
Stage Fright (1984)
Bummer Summer (1983)

Martin's Major Literary Awards

2003 Newbery Honor Book
   A Corner of the Universe

books about a babysitting cooperative. The editor asked Martin to write four books for the series. The books were popular, and Martin was asked to write two more books for the series. Those books were very popular, too, and many copies were sold. "That was when we decided that we really had something," Martin says.

Martin is the author of almost all the books in the Baby-Sitters Club and Baby-Sitters Little Sister series. When she first began writing the series, she would write two books each month. She now has other authors help her write books for the series.

> *"I write books as pure entertainment for myself, as well as for the kids, but I hope that avid readers . . . are reading other things, too, and I also hope that reluctant readers who get hooked on reading through series reading . . . will then 'graduate' to other kinds of books."*

Currently, Martin writes three-quarters of the books published each year in both series. Even though she does not write all the books, she outlines the chapters of each book. She also edits the books before they are published.

In her writing, Martin relies on her memory. She can remember things that happened to her as a young girl. She uses these memories in her books. "When I speak through my young characters, I am remembering and reliving," she

MARTIN BASED THE BOOK *STAGE FRIGHT* ON HER
OWN STAGE FRIGHT SHE EXPERIENCED AS A CHILD.

notes. "Redoing all those things one is never supposed to be able to redo."

Along with her writing, Martin is active in supporting community programs. She also supports a dance program at an elementary school in New York City. She continues to write books and lives with her pets in Upstate New York.

> *"I think one has to keep in mind exactly what kids are going to be getting out of the books. Children, no matter what anybody thinks, are very vulnerable."*

WHERE TO FIND OUT MORE ABOUT ANN M. MARTIN

BOOKS

Kovacs, Deborah, and James Preller. *Meet the Authors and Illustrators: 60 Creators of Favorite Children's Books Talk about Their Work.* Vol. 2. New York: Scholastic, 1993.

Silvey, Anita, ed. *The Essential Guide to Children's Books and Their Creators.* Boston: Houghton Mifflin Company, 2002.

WEB SITES

KIDSREADS.COM
http://www.kidsreads.com/authors/au-martin-ann.asp
To read a biographical sketch of Ann M. Martin

SCHOLASTIC ONLINE AUTHORS
http://www.scholastic.com/annmartin/index.htm
To read letters from Ann M. Martin to her fans

MARTIN HAD MANY PETS WHEN SHE WAS A CHILD. AT ONE POINT, NINE CATS WERE LIVING AT HER HOUSE!

Bill Martin Jr.

Born: March 20, 1916
Died: August 11, 2004

For nearly six decades, Bill Martin Jr. crafted hundreds of books that were hits with parents and kids alike. What makes his books so good? Martin chose each and every word carefully. He spoke his sentences aloud before he wrote them down, making sure that each one had the perfect rhythm and the best possible sound. Martin's careful choice of words helped to make him one of the most successful and popular children's picture book authors.

William Ivan Martin was born on March 20, 1916, in Hiawatha, Kansas. Even though there weren't many books around the house when Bill was growing up, he heard lots of great stories. Bill's parents and his grandmother were all excellent storytellers. Bill was fascinated by their magical tales.

MARTIN APPEARED ON TWO EDUCATIONAL TELEVISION SERIES:
STORY TELLER (1955) AND *BILL MARTIN* (1968).

In elementary school, Bill's love of listening continued. His favorite teacher, Miss Davis, read to her students constantly. Even when story time was over, Miss Davis would continue reading if her students asked her to.

Although Bill loved listening to stories, he didn't like to read them. Martin said he was a nonreader until he went to

> *"A blessed thing happened to me when I was a child. I had a teacher who read to me."*

college. There, with the help of caring teachers, the young man learned the joys of reading. Martin's favorite things to read were poems. He memorized works by Stephen Vincent Benét and Robert Frost, repeating them aloud to others. Martin graduated from college and began teaching high school journalism, drama, and English classes.

During World War II (1939–1945), Martin entered the air force. He served as a newspaper reporter and got his first writing experience. When Martin returned to Kansas, he and his brother Bernard decided to team up and create a children's book. *Little Squeegy Bug* featured words by Bill and pictures by Bernard. When they couldn't find a publisher for the book, the two brothers published their work themselves. Over the next eight years, they wrote and published seventeen books together.

Martin went back to college in Chicago to learn more about children and reading. While he was studying, he also worked as an elementary

WILLIAM IVAN MARTIN WAS NAMED FOR BOTH HIS FATHER (WILLIAM) AND HIS MOTHER (IVA). IN COLLEGE, WHEN BILL WOULDN'T REVEAL HIS MIDDLE NAME, HE WAS LISTED AS BILL MARTIN JR. THE NAME STUCK.

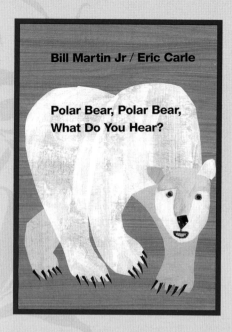

Bill Martin Jr / Eric Carle

Polar Bear, Polar Bear, What Do You Hear?

A Selected Bibliography of Martin's Work

Little Granny Quarterback (with Michael Sampson, 2001)

Rock It, Sock It, Number Line (with Michael Sampson, 2001)

Chicken Chuck (with Bernard Martin, 2000)

A Beasty Story (with Steven Kellogg, 1999)

Swish! (with Michael Sampson, 1997)

Polar Bear, Polar Bear, What Do You Hear? (1991)

Chicka Chicka Boom Boom (with John Archambault, 1989)

The Magic Pumpkin (with John Archambault, 1989)

Knots on a Counting Rope (with John Archambault, 1987)

Barn Dance! (with John Archambault, 1986)

White Dynamite & Curly Kidd (with John Archambault, 1986)

The Ghost-Eye Tree (with John Archambault, 1985)

Here Are My Hands (with John Archambault, 1985)

Brown Bear, Brown Bear, What Do You See? (1970)

Little Squeegy Bug (with Bernard Martin, 1945)

Martin's Major Literary Award

1990 Boston Globe–Horn Book Picture Book Honor Book
  Chicka Chicka Boom Boom

school principal. In 1961, Martin moved to New York City to become a textbook editor. As an editor, he helped create reading, social studies, science, and math programs for kids.

When Martin began to write full-time, his love of listening helped him out. Martin had a good ear for fun words and fine language. He knew a terrific story when he told one, too. Martin always said that he didn't write books—he spoke them.

One of Martin's most famous books is *Brown Bear, Brown Bear, What Do You See?*

> *"The love of language conquered my fear of the written word."*

Martin got the idea for Brown Bear when he was riding on a train. By the time the thirty-minute trip was over, he had planned the entire book in his head.

When Martin wasn't writing, he liked to sing folk songs as well as travel around the nation, giving speeches to young and old who admired his gift as a master storyteller. Martin lived in Commerce, Texas, until his death in 2004.

❧

WHERE TO FIND OUT MORE ABOUT BILL MARTIN JR.

BOOKS

Kovacs, Deborah, and James Preller. *Meet the Authors and Illustrators: 60 Creators of Favorite Children's Books Talk about Their Work.* Vol. 2. New York: Scholastic, 1993.

McElmeel, Sharron L. *100 Most Popular Picture Book Authors and Illustrators: Biographical Sketches and Bibliographies.* Englewood, Colo.: Libraries Unlimited, 2000.

Silvey, Anita, ed. *The Essential Guide to Children's Books and Their Creators.* Boston: Houghton Mifflin Company, 2002.

WEB SITE

BILL MARTIN JR. AND MICHAEL SAMPSON HOME PAGE
http://www.tiill.com/bill.htm
To read a biographical sketch of Bill Martin Jr. and information about his books

---

THE BILL MARTIN JR. LIBRARY IS LOCATED AT TEXAS A&M UNIVERSITY IN COMMERCE, TEXAS. THE LIBRARY, WHICH OPENED IN SEPTEMBER 2000, HOLDS MANY OF MARTIN'S BOOKS, MANUSCRIPTS, AND LETTERS.

Mercer Mayer

Born: December 10, 1943

Mercer Mayer was born on December 30, 1943, in Little Rock, Arkansas, while his father was serving in World War II (1939–1945). Mercer was already about two years old when he first met his father. Mercer's father was in the U.S. Navy, so the family moved many times. Mercer and his family finally settled in Hawaii.

As a young boy, Mercer loved to draw. He enjoyed looking at illustrated books, too. "I was in love with the world, or should I say worlds, they depicted," Mayer remembers. "Pen and ink was always quite magical for me and still is. I was amazed that a bottle of black ink and a scratchy pen point could create such wonderful things."

MAYER IS ONE OF THE FIRST AUTHORS TO CREATE WORDLESS PICTURE BOOKS.

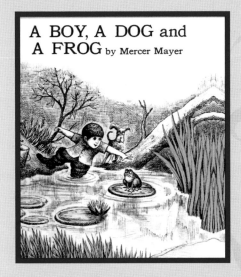

After graduating from high school, Mercer Mayer went to the Honolulu Academy of Arts. His art instructors were impressed with his talent, but they discouraged him from becoming a book illustrator.

In 1964, Mayer moved to New York City to continue his art studies. He was still interested in working as a book illustrator.

He showed his portfolio of drawings to many publishers, but he was not able to find a job. "Finally I received some

"Now I'm a big kid and I write about things that happen now, especially with my own children. They always remind me of what it was like."

A Selected Bibliography of Mayer's Work

Little Drummer Mouse: A Christmas Story (2006)
There Are Monsters Everywhere (2005)
Harvest Time (2004)
Beach Day (2003)
The Mixed-Up Morning (2002)
Camping Out (2001)
Little Critter's the Best Present (2000)
Just a Bully (with Gina Mayer, 1999)
The Figure in the Shadows (Illustrations only, 1993)
Thrills and Spills (1991)
Appelard and Liverwurst (1978)
Little Monster's Neighborhood (1978)
Everyone Knows What a Dragon Looks Like (Illustrations only, 1976)
Liza Lou and the Yeller Belly Swamp (1976)
Professor Wormbog in Search of the Zipperump-a-Zoo (1976)
The Great Cat Chase: A Wordless Book (1975)
Just for You (1975)
Walk, Robot, Walk (1974)
What Do You Do with a Kangaroo? (1974)
Frog on His Own (1973)
A Silly Story (1972)
The Queen Always Wanted to Dance (1971)
A Special Trick (1970)
Frog, Where Are You? (1969)
I Am a Hunter (1969)
There's a Nightmare in My Closet (1968)
If I Had . . . (1968)
Terrible Troll (1968)
A Boy, a Dog and a Frog (1967)

good advice from an art director," Mayer says. "He told me to throw my portfolio away because it was so bad."

Mayer was disappointed, but he decided to take the advice. He found a job with an advertising agency and worked on improving his illustration skills.

After his skills improved, Mayer was asked to illustrate several children's books. He also created drawings for his own first book, *A Boy, a Dog and a Frog*. This book was published in 1967. It was a picture book that did not include any words. Mayer has incorporated words in many of the books that he has created since that time.

"Most of my books are about things that happened to me when I was a little kid," Mayer explains. He writes stories and creates illustrations from a child's point of view. This style makes his books more interesting to children. Some of his best-known books are in the Little Critter and Little Monster series.

> *"I didn't really want to be an artist. Originally, I wanted to be an astronomer—actually, I wanted to ride a UFO and go to Mars."*

Mayer continues to work on writing and illustrating his own books. He also finds time to illustrate books written by other authors.

Mercer Mayer has four children and lives in Connecticut. "It's real fun to be an old kid," says Mayer.

MAYER DESCRIBES HIS CHILDHOOD AS BEING VERY MUCH LIKE THE CHILDHOOD OF TOM SAWYER, THE FICTIONAL CHARACTER CREATED BY MARK TWAIN.

❧

WHERE TO FIND OUT MORE ABOUT MERCER MAYER

BOOKS

De Montreville, Doris, and Elizabeth D. Crawford, eds. *Fourth Book of Junior Authors & Illustrators.* New York: H. W. Wilson Company, 1978.

McElmeel, Sharron L. *100 Most Popular Picture Book Authors and Illustrators: Biographical Sketches and Bibliographies.* Englewood, Colo.: Libraries Unlimited, 2000.

Silvey, Anita, ed. *Children's Books and Their Creators.* Boston: Houghton Mifflin, 1995.

WEB SITES

HARPERCHILDRENS.COM: MERCER MAYER
http://www.harperchildrens.com/catalog/author_xml.asp?authorid=17622
To read a short biography of Mercer Mayer and to see a gallery of his many books

THE OFFICIAL LITTLE CRITTER WEB SITE
http://www.littlecritter.com/
To read about the Little Critter characters, view an online movie, and access coloring pages related to the series

MAYER HAS ALWAYS BEEN FASCINATED BY BLACK-AND-WHITE PEN-AND-INK DRAWINGS.

Robert McCloskey

Born: September 15, 1914
Died: June 30, 2003

Robert McCloskey was well known for his children's books about real-life people and places. Three of his best-known books are *Make Way for Ducklings, Homer Price,* and *Blueberries for Sal.* But McCloskey didn't plan on being a writer. Before writing children's books, he had many other interests.

Robert McCloskey was born on September 15, 1914, in Hamilton, Ohio. As a child, he loved music. He began by taking piano lessons. Soon, he was also playing harmonica, oboe, and drums.

Robert also developed an interest in mechanical things. He wanted to know how machines worked. He tried his own mechanical inventions.

As he got older, Robert discovered art. He began drawing for his high school newspaper. He was so good that he won a scholarship to study at Boston's Vesper George School of Art after high school. At that

---

MCCLOSKEY WAS THE FIRST PERSON TO WIN TWO CALDECOTT MEDALS.

point, it seemed that McCloskey would focus on a career as an artist. He continued to study art at the National Academy of Design in New York and privately with an artist on Cape Cod, Massachusetts.

McCloskey received some advice from a children's book editor in New York. McCloskey showed her drawings he had done of characters from fantasy and mythology. She was not very impressed. She suggested that he focus on the things in the real world. He needed to pay attention to what went on around him and to center his art on real characters and events.

During the next several years, McCloskey took her advice. He wrote a book about a boy who played the harmonica. This boy could have been McCloskey himself! The book was called *Lentil* and was published in 1940.

Make Way for Ducklings was McCloskey's next book. It took him almost three years to complete it. It was important that he draw and write about the ducks accurately. So one day he bought four live ducks. He brought them home and followed them around his apartment for the next few weeks.

Many of McCloskey's books are based on real people and on events in his own life. *Homer Price* gave McCloskey an opportunity to think

"It is just sort of an accident that I write books. I really think up stories in pictures and just fill in the pictures with a sentence or a paragraph or a few pages of words."

MCCLOSKEY GOT THE IDEA FOR *MAKE WAY FOR DUCKLINGS* WHEN HE WAS LIVING IN BOSTON AND SAW REAL DUCKS GETTING IN THE WAY OF TRAFFIC AROUND THE BOSTON PUBLIC GARDEN.

A Selected Bibliography of McCloskey's Work

Burt Dow, Deep-Water Man: A Tale of the Sea in the Classic Tradition (1963)

Time of Wonder (1957)

Journey Cake, Ho! (1953)

One Morning in Maine (1952)

Centerburg Tales (1951)

Blueberries for Sal (1948)

Homer Price (1943)

Make Way for Ducklings (1941)

Lentil (1940)

McCloskey's Major Literary Awards

1958 Caldecott Medal
Time of Wonder

1954 Caldecott Honor Book
Journey Cake, Ho

1953 Caldecott Honor Book
One Morning in Maine

1949 Caldecott Honor Book
Blueberries for Sal

1942 Caldecott Medal
Make Way for Ducklings

back on his childhood experiences in the Midwest. In *Blueberries for Sal,* McCloskey based the main character, Sal, on his daughter Sarah. The sequel, *One Morning in Maine,* includes a character, Jane, based on his second daughter, who has the same name. Both stories reflect the McCloskey family's experiences living in Maine.

McCloskey's books are known for their heartwarming stories and illustrations. He felt strongly about the role of art both in his books and in the world of children. McCloskey said, "It is important that we develop people who can make worthwhile pictures, and it is important that we teach people to 'read' these pictures. That is why, in my opinion, every child, along with learning to read and write, should be taught to draw and to design."

After entertaining readers for generations, McCloskey died on Deer Isle, Maine, at the age of eighty-eight.

> *"I get a lot of letters. Not only from children but from adults, too. Almost every week, every month, clippings come in from some part of the world where ducks are crossing the street."*

WHERE TO FIND OUT MORE ABOUT ROBERT MCCLOSKEY

BOOKS

Kovacs, Deborah, and James Preller. *Meet the Authors and Illustrators: 60 Creators of Favorite Children's Books Talk about Their Work.* Vol. 1. New York: Scholastic, 1991.

McElmeel, Sharron L. *100 Most Popular Picture Book Authors and Illustrators: Biographical Sketches and Bibliographies.* Englewood, Colo.: Libraries Unlimited, 2000.

Rockman, Connie C., ed. *The Ninth Book of Junior Authors and Illustrators.* New York: H. W. Wilson Company, 2004.

WEB SITES

OHIO READING ROADTRIP
http://www.ohioreadingroadtrip.org/mccloskey/
To read a biography of one of Ohio's most famous authors

THE SCOOP
http://www.friend.ly.net/users/jorban/biographies/mccloskeyrobert/
To read a biographical sketch of and a booklist for Robert McCloskey

LARGER-THAN-LIFE BRONZE STATUES OF MCCLOSKEY'S MOTHER DUCK AND DUCKLINGS WERE PLACED IN THE BOSTON PUBLIC GARDEN IN HONOR OF MCCLOSKEY'S AWARD-WINNING BOOK.

Emily Arnold McCully

Born: July 1, 1939

When Emily Arnold McCully was a child, almost all the stories she read had male heroes. But in the stories McCully writes, girls are always having adventures. In her most famous book, *Mirette on the High Wire,* a young girl becomes an expert tightrope walker. Mirette's determination and bravery give Bellini, the world's greatest

high-wire walker, the courage to return to the wire. McCully illustrated the story with vivid watercolor paintings.

Emily Arnold McCully was born on July 1, 1939, in Galesburg, Illinois. When she was young, she and her family moved to Garden City, New York, not far from New York City. Like her character Mirette, Emily was something of a daredevil, often climbing trees and buildings in search of adventure.

MCCULLY LOVES THEATER AS MUCH AS SHE LOVES CHILDREN'S BOOKS. IN COLLEGE, SHE WROTE AN AWARD-WINNING MUSICAL. SHE HAS ALSO WORKED AS A PROFESSIONAL ACTRESS.

Even as a very small child, Emily loved books. She started reading at age three. She also loved drawing and often came up with stories and pictures that she made into books. Her mother believed in her talent and always encouraged her. She urged Emily to keep practicing until she could draw things perfectly.

In school, Emily did many art projects. She designed posters, concert programs, and sets for plays. By the time she was in high school, she was traveling into New York City by herself. She would go to museums and sketch people on the street. "The city fueled my ambitions for an active life in the arts," she says.

A Selected Bibliography of McCully's Work

Mattie's Invention (2006)
School (2005)
Squirrel and John Muir (2004)
Katie's Wish (Illustrations only, 2003)
Sing a Song of Piglets: A Calendar in Verse (Illustrations only, 2002)
Four Hungry Kittens (2001)
The Orphan Singer (2001)
Ten Go Tango (Illustrations only, 2000)
Mouse Practice (1999)
Beautiful Warrior: The Legend of the Nun's Kung Fu (1998)
An Outlaw Thanksgiving (1998)
Popcorn at the Palace (1997)
Starring Mirette and Bellini (1997)
The Ballot Box Battle (1996)
The Bobbin Girl (1996)
Little Kit; or, the Industrious Flea Circus Girl (1995)
Grandmas at Bat (1993)
Mirette on the High Wire (1992)
The Grandma Mix-Up: Stories and Pictures (1988)
Picnic (1984)
Black Is Brown Is Tan (Illustrations only, 1973)
How to Eat Fried Worms (Illustrations only, 1973)
Journey from Peppermint Street (Illustrations only, 1968)
Sea Beach Express (Illustrations only, 1966)

McCully's Major Literary Awards

1993 Caldecott Medal
 Mirette on the High Wire

McCully studied art history at Brown University in Rhode Island. She later earned a master's degree from Columbia University in New York City. After college, she got a job working in an advertising agency. When this didn't seem like it was going to turn into a career, she showed some of her drawings to art directors at publishing houses. Gradually, she began getting jobs designing covers for books.

Then one day, an editor saw a poster she had made hanging in a New York City subway station. The editor tracked her down and asked her if she wanted to illustrate a book. It was *Sea Beach Express,* written by George Panetta, and it was the beginning of her career in children's books. Since then, McCully has illustrated about 200 books for other authors, including *How to Eat Fried Worms,* by Thomas Rockwell, and *Black Is Brown Is Tan,* by Arnold Adoff.

"My advice for aspiring artists and writers is this: Don't worry about what other people are doing. . . . Work from what is inside you, crying out— however softly, however timidly—for expression."

McCully did not create a children's book of her own until 1984, almost twenty years after she began illustrating other people's books. Called *Picnic,* it is a wordless book about a family of mice. Since then, McCully has written many easy-reader books, including *Grandmas at Bat* and *The Grandma Mix-Up: Stories and Pictures.* But most often, she writes for older children.

ALL OF BELLINI'S HIGH-WIRE FEATS IN McCULLY'S BOOKS ARE BASED ON THOSE OF A REAL HIGH-WIRE WALKER NAMED BLONDIN. BLONDIN EVEN COOKED EGGS WHILE STANDING ON A WIRE STRETCHED ACROSS NIAGARA FALLS.

McCully enjoys writing about historical subjects. *The Bobbin Girl* is about a ten-year-old working in a textile factory in the early 1800s, and *The Orphan Singer* is about a girl who becomes a famous singer in eighteenth-century Italy. As long as McCully keeps coming across interesting historic characters, she will always have material for more books.

"Part of the courage it takes to be an author—or to do anything worth doing—is to risk rejection and to risk failure."

WHERE TO FIND OUT MORE ABOUT EMILY ARNOLD McCULLY

BOOKS

Silvey, Anita, ed. *The Essential Guide to Children's Books and Their Creators.* Boston: Houghton Mifflin Company, 2002.

Sutherland, Zena. *Children and Books.* New York: Addison Wesley Longman, 1997.

WEB SITES
CHILDREN'S LITERATURE
http://www.childrenslit.com/f_mccully.html
To read an autobiographical sketch of Emily Arnold McCully

THOUGH McCULLY IS FAMOUS FOR THE WATERCOLOR PAINTINGS IN HER BOOKS, SHE ONLY BEGAN PAINTING IN 1992. BEFORE THAT, SHE ALWAYS DREW PICTURES WITH A PEN AND THEN FILLED IN THE COLOR.

Gerald McDermott

Born: January 31, 1941

erald McDermott wanted to be a filmmaker. He studied film-making for several years, and he even made several films for children that were successful. He was then asked to create books for children from stories in his films. Since then, he has written and illustrated several books from his films. His best-known books include *The Magic Tree: A Tale from the Congo, The Stonecutter: A Japanese Folk Tale,* and *The Knight of the Lion.*

Gerald McDermott was born on January 31, 1941, in Detroit, Michigan. When Gerald was about four years old, his parents noticed his talent for art. He was very good at drawing and painting pictures. They enrolled him in art classes at the Detroit Institute of Arts. He attended classes every Saturday until he was a teenager.

———

MCDERMOTT'S FILM *ANANSI THE SPIDER* WON THE
1970 AMERICAN FILM FESTIVAL BLUE RIBBON.

When he was nine years old, Gerald appeared on a radio show. He was one of the actors in a folktale performance. This experience taught Gerald many things. He learned about the technical parts of doing a performance. He also learned how to work with actors. This experience was helpful to him when he became a filmmaker later in life.

Gerald attended a high school in Detroit that had a special arts curriculum. He studied art, music, and dance. He wanted to study filmmaking, but the school did not have any film courses. So he began to make films on his own. He also got a part-time job creating backgrounds for a television animation studio.

In 1959, McDermott won a scholarship to attend an art school in New York. But this school did

"Every Saturday, from early childhood through early adolescence, was spent in those halls [in the Detroit Institute of Arts]. I virtually lived in the museum, drawing and painting and coming to know the works of that great collection. I've kept a brush in my hand ever since."

not have any courses in filmmaking, either. Instead of going to school, McDermott took a job as a graphic designer for a television station. He went back to school about one year later. For the next several years, McDermott spent most of his time making films for children. All his films were animated and took a great deal of time to create.

McDERMOTT'S ANIMATED FILMS REQUIRED HIM TO DRAW **6,000** INDIVIDUAL PICTURES. THE PICTURES— OR FRAMES—WERE FILMED AND ACCOMPANIED BY MUSIC.

A Selected Bibliography of McDermott's Work

Creation (2003)

Jabutí the Tortoise: A Trickster Tale from the Amazon (2001)

The Fox and the Stork (1999)

Musicians of the Sun (1997)

Raven: A Trickster Tale from the Pacific Northwest (1993)

Zomo the Rabbit: A Trickster Tale from West Africa (1992)

Marcel the Pastry Chef (Illustrations only, 1991)

Tim O'Toole and the Wee Folk: An Irish Tale (1990)

Daniel O'Rourke: An Irish Tale (1986)

Daughter of Earth: A Roman Myth (1984)

Carlo Collodi's The Adventures of Pinocchio (Illustrations only, 1981)

Papagayo: The Mischief Maker (1980)

The Knight of the Lion (1979)

The Voyage of Osiris: A Myth of Ancient Egypt (1977)

The Stonecutter: A Japanese Folk Tale (1975)

Arrow to the Sun: A Pueblo Indian Tale (1974)

The Magic Tree: A Tale from the Congo (1973)

Anansi the Spider: A Tale from the Ashanti (1972)

McDermott's Major Literary Awards

1994 Caldecott Honor Book

1993 Boston Globe–Horn Book Picture Book Honor Book
   Raven: A Trickster Tale from the Pacific Northwest

1975 Caldecott Medal
   Arrow to the Sun: A Pueblo Indian Tale

1973 Boston Globe–Horn Book Picture Book Honor Book
   The Magic Tree: A Tale from the Congo

1973 Caldecott Honor Book
   Anansi the Spider: A Tale from the Ashanti

McDermott enjoyed making films, but he was discouraged because he was not making much money. He and his wife, an author and illustrator of children's books, decided to move to France. Before they moved, he met with his wife's publisher. McDermott was hired to create children's books from his movies. McDermott found this to be an interesting

"It has been my experience that even the youngest children respond in a direct and receptive manner to the most stylized of images. I believe this quality is manifested in the magic and symbolism of their own paintings."

challenge. This began a new career for McDermott as a children's book author and illustrator. His first book, *Anansi the Spider: A Tale from the Ashanti,* was published in 1972. He has since written and illustrated several other children's books based on folktales.

McDermott continues to write and illustrate books for children and young people. He lives with his wife in New York.

❧

WHERE TO FIND OUT MORE ABOUT GERALD MCDERMOTT

BOOKS

De Montreville, Doris, and Elizabeth D. Crawford, eds. *Fourth Book of Junior Authors & Illustrators.* New York: H. W. Wilson Company, 1978.

Silvey, Anita, ed. *The Essential Guide to Children's Books and Their Creators.* Boston: Houghton Mifflin Company, 2002.

WEB SITE

GERALD MCDERMOTT HOME PAGE
http://www.geraldmcdermott.com/
To read a biographical sketch of Gerald McDermott,
and for information about his books

———

MANY OF MCDERMOTT'S BOOKS HAVE BEEN PUBLISHED IN JAPAN.
HE HAS TRAVELED THROUGHOUT JAPAN GIVING SPEECHES ABOUT HIS WORK.

Megan McDonald

Born: February 28, 1959

Author Megan McDonald knows what it's like to have some bad days. Growing up with four bossy older sisters, Megan definitely had a few. But Megan's childhood experiences came in handy when she began creating fiction stories for children. Her strong and sassy kid characters and their amazing adventures attract readers of all ages.

Megan McDonald was born on February 28, 1959, in Pittsburgh, Pennsylvania. Her father was an iron-worker, and her mother was a social worker. Megan and her sisters grew up surrounded by books and stories.

Megan's father was a great storyteller who would make up stories about anything—even designs he saw in the peanut butter or the ice

---

MCDONALD HAS HAD MANY PETS, INCLUDING SNAKES, TURTLES, AND NEWTS.

cream. At dinner, Megan, her parents, and her sisters would gather in the kitchen to swap stories about their day.

As the youngest child, Megan had a tough time getting a word in edgewise. To give her the chance to freely express herself, Megan's mother bought her a journal to write in.

Although Megan's sisters took control of the talking, they also introduced her to the world of books. They taught her to check the end of a book first to make sure she wanted to read the whole thing. If the ending made Megan cry, then the book was worth reading. Megan's sisters also let her tag along when the bookmobile was in the neighborhood. Megan

A Selected Bibliography of McDonald's Work

Daisy Jane, Best-ever Flower Girl (2007)

Stink and the Incredible Super-Galactic Jawbreaker (2006)

Saving the Liberty Bell (2005)

Judy Moody, M.D.: The Doctor is In! (2004)

Penguin and Little Blue (2003)

Judy Moody Saves the World (2002)

Judy Moody Gets Famous (2001)

Reptiles Are My Life (2001)

Beezy and Funnybone (2000)

Lucky Star (2000)

Shadows in the Glasshouse (2000)

Bedbugs (1999)

The Bone Keeper (1999)

Insects Are My Life (1999)

Judy Moody (1999)

The Night Iguana Left Home (1999)

Beezy at Bat (1998)

Beezy Magic (1998)

Beezy (1997)

Tundra Mouse: A Storyknife Tale (1997)

My House Has Stars (1996)

The Bridge to Nowhere (1993)

The Great Pumpkin Switch (1992)

Whoo-oo Is It? (1992)

The Potato Man (1991)

Is This a House for Hermit Crab? (1990)

always checked out the same book, a biography of Virginia Dare. Finally, Megan was banned from taking out the book so that other kids could have the chance to read it.

As a teenager, Megan enjoyed books and stories. When she was fourteen, Megan worked at a local library. As an adult, she took jobs that kept her connected to books and to children. Over the years, McDonald has worked as a librarian, a park ranger, a museum guide, and a storyteller. She put her first story on paper in 1990, when she completed *Is This a House for Hermit Crab?* Four years later, McDonald left her job as a librarian and began writing full-time.

McDonald gets many of the ideas for stories from her own memories and experiences. Both the Beezy books and the Judy Moody books, for example, feature events from McDonald's childhood. When McDonald wrote the first Judy Moody book, she used herself as the model for the title character. But McDonald made Judy the oldest so that she could finally have a shot at being the boss!

"What I like about writing is that in all things there is a story—a leaf falling, . . . a child on the way to school, a stranger on the bus, something found in the street. One begins to see differently, and each new thing takes on an aspect of story."

Some of McDonald's books are based on stories her father

McDONALD WAS IN THE FIFTH GRADE WHEN SHE WROTE HER FIRST STORY. CALLED "THE PLEA OF THE PENCIL SHARPENER," IT WAS ABOUT LIFE FROM A PENCIL SHARPENER'S POINT OF VIEW.

told her and her sisters when they were young. *The Potato Man* and *The Great Pumpkin Switch* are two such books. They are based on tales about her father's childhood in Pittsburgh during the Great Depression.

"Connecting children with books has always been the centerpiece of my life's work."

One of McDonald's favorite things about being a writer is to put herself into her characters' shoes. She enjoys spending the day thinking like a mouse or like a girl from colonial times. McDonald says she can get an idea from just about anything.

McDonald lives in California with her husband, Richard. She enjoys visiting schools, where she tells stories and talks about her books.

WHERE TO FIND OUT MORE ABOUT MEGAN MCDONALD

BOOKS
Holtze, Sally Holmes, ed. *Seventh Book of Junior Authors & Illustrators.* New York: H. W. Wilson Company, 1996.

WEB SITES
MEGAN MCDONALD HOME PAGE
www.meganmcdonald.net
To read more about Megan McDonald and to take a tour of her studio

VISITINGAUTHORS.COM
http://visitingauthors.com/authors/mcdonald_megan/mcdonald_megan_bio.html
To read a biographical sketch of and a booklist for Megan McDonald

IN ONE OF MCDONALD'S BOOKS, SHE INVENTED A CREATURE CALLED A PRICKLEPINE FISH. MCDONALD HAS RECEIVED LETTERS FROM KIDS ACROSS THE COUNTRY SAYING THAT THEY'VE SPOTTED THIS MAKE-BELIEVE ANIMAL.

Ann McGovern

Born: May 25, 1930

Whether she is writing about history, exotic animals, or famous people, Ann McGovern makes her subjects exciting. She is the author of more than fifty children's books, and many are based on her own travel adventures.

Ann McGovern was born Ann Weinberger in 1930 in New York City. Her father died when she was only five. Even though Ann had an older sister, she often felt sad and lonely. She also suffered from a severe stutter.

Since she couldn't express herself well by speaking, Ann poured her thoughts and feelings into reading and writing. Her favorite books were fairy tales and travel adventures. When Ann was eight, she began writing. She spent hours in the library or perched in a tree

---

MCGOVERN HAS CONDUCTED POETRY WRITING WORKSHOPS AT A WOMEN'S PRISON IN BEDFORD HILLS, NEW YORK.

in New York City's Central Park. In these sheltered surroundings, the shy, unhappy girl wrote countless stories and poems. "I always felt better about myself after writing," she recalls.

Ann attended public schools in New York City. She was so shy that she rarely spoke in class. Ann found history classes disappointing because, in her opinion, history was taught in such a boring way. Later, as an author, she resolved to write truly interesting books about life in the past.

> *"Making a difference in children's lives is why I plan to write till I'm ninety!"*

> *"Books can be an escape hatch from a troubled childhood, a window to a world of possibilities, a meeting of inspiring heroes and heroines, surprising soul mates that change a life, and spur creativity; they were all these for me and more."*

When it was time for college, she headed west to attend the University of New Mexico in Albuquerque. She married her English teacher and became Ann McGovern. The couple's son, Peter, was born in 1950 and was just a baby when the marriage ended in divorce. McGovern then returned to New York City.

Supporting herself and her son was rough. At first, McGovern lived in a fifth-floor, walk-up apartment that had only cold water. To make ends meet, she worked as a waitress and a model. She also tried her hand at writing, and

McGOVERN HAS TRAVELED TO ALL SEVEN CONTINENTS. MANY OF HER BOOKS ARE ILLUSTRATED WITH PHOTOGRAPHS TAKEN DURING THESE ADVENTURES.

A Selected Bibliography of McGovern's Work

If You Lived in the Days of the Knights (2001)

Playing with the Penguins and Other Adventures in Antarctica (1994)

Down Under, Down Under: Diving Adventures on the Great Barrier Reef (1989)

Stone Soup (1986)

Night Dive (1984)

Elephant Baby: The Story of Little Tembo (1982)

Great Gorillas (1980)

Shark Lady: True Adventures of Eugenie Clark (1978)

Sharks (1976)

If You Lived with the Sioux Indians (1974)

Scram, Kid! (1974)

If You Lived in Colonial Times (1966)

Runaway Slave: The Story of Harriet Tubman (1965)

Aesop's Fables (1963)

Annie Oakley and the Rustlers (1955)

Roy Rogers and the Mountain Lion (1955)

McGovern's Major Literary Award

1975 Boston Globe–Horn Book Picture Book Honor Book
   Scram, Kid!

her first books—*Annie Oakley and the Rustlers* and *Roy Rogers and the Mountain Lion*—were published in 1955. McGovern also wrote several Little Golden Books during the 1950s.

In 1958, McGovern began working for Scholastic Book Services as the associate editor of the Arrow Book Club. She went on to become the founder and editor of Scholastic's See Saw Book Club in 1965. By that time, she had written several more children's books. Finally, in 1967, she became a full-time writer.

In the 1960s, McGovern began writing her If You Lived series. These books show what life was like for people of different cultures and historic periods. Typical titles in the series are *If You Lived in Colonial Times* and *If You Lived in the Days of the Knights.*

In 1970, McGovern married Martin Scheiner, an engineer with three children. He introduced her to sailing, scuba diving, and world travel. Her travel adventures inspired many new books on undersea life and wild animals around the world. Sadly, Scheiner died in 1992, but McGovern's love for travel lives on.

McGovern has also written biographies, folktales, fiction stories, and poetry. When she is not traveling, she lives in New York City.

❧

WHERE TO FIND OUT MORE ABOUT ANN MCGOVERN

BOOK
De Montreville, Doris, and Elizabeth D. Crawford, eds. *Fourth Book of Junior Authors and Illustrators.* New York: H. W. Wilson, 1978.

WEB SITES
ANN MCGOVERN
http://www.annmcgovern.com/
For an autobiography of the writer

MEET THE AUTHOR
http://books.scholastic.com/teachers/authorsandbooks/authorstudies/authorhome.jsp?author ID=148&&displayName=Biography
For a biography of the author plus a link to her books

MCGOVERN HAS GONE SCUBA DIVING AMONG SHARKS OFF THE COAST OF AUSTRALIA.

Patricia McKissack

Born: August 9, 1944

To write the story of a person is to give him or her a voice, to ensure that the person is not forgotten, to remember the person's accomplishments. When Patricia McKissack was teaching junior high school students in Kirkwood, Missouri, she wanted to teach them about the poet Paul Laurence Dunbar. There were no books on Dunbar for children. Believing that Dunbar's story needed to be told, McKissack wrote his biography herself.

She was born Patricia Carwell on August 9, 1944, just outside of Nashville, Tennessee. At that time, segregation still prevented African Americans in the South from sharing the liberties of whites. Patricia's parents worked for the government, and Patricia herself believed that the government could be the agent of good.

She attended the Tennessee Agricultural and Industrial State University during the early 1960s. It was a time, she recalls, when

IN 1987, LINDENWOOD COLLEGE IN ST. CHARLES, MISSOURI, OPENED THE McKISSACK CENTER FOR BLACK CHILDREN'S LITERATURE. IT HOUSES THE COMPLETE WORKS OF McKISSACK, HER HUSBAND, AND OTHER AFRICAN AMERICAN AUTHORS.

black Americans were beginning to hope. President John F. Kennedy denounced segregation and all forms of racism. His words and his call for Americans to take action in shaping a more just society were inspiring.

> "We were very idealistic. That was the period in which African Americans were really looking up, coming out of darkness, segregation, and discrimination, and the doors were beginning to open."

Patricia Carwell took action. She participated in sit-ins in segregated restaurants and other businesses. Sit-ins were designed to protest peacefully the fact that blacks were not permitted into those businesses. One of her fellow protesters was Fredrick McKissack, who had also grown up in Nashville. The two were married in 1964. They have three sons.

Another form of action Patricia McKissack took was writing. She had been inspired by Kennedy's words, and she wanted to inspire others with her own stories. She wrote biographies, often with her husband, of African American civil rights leaders, athletes, entertainers, and artists. She wrote about the forgotten contributions African Americans made to American society.

In 1975, McKissack earned a master's degree in early childhood literature from Webster University in St. Louis, Missouri. She has been a junior high school English teacher and a part-time college instructor.

IN *RED-TAIL ANGELS: THE STORY OF THE TUSKEGEE AIRMEN OF WORLD WAR II,* MCKISSACK PROFILED A CORPS OF AFRICAN AMERICAN AVIATORS WHO WERE NOT ALLOWED TO SERVE WITH THEIR WHITE COMRADES.

A Selected Bibliography of McKissack's Work

Days of Jubilee: The End of Slavery in the United States (with Fredrick McKissack, 2003)

Black Hands, White Sails: The Story of African-American Whalers (with Fredrick McKissack, 1999)

Rebels against Slavery: American Slave Revolts (with Fredrick McKissack, 1996)

Red-Tail Angels: The Story of the Tuskegee Airmen of World War II (1996)

Christmas in the Big House, Christmas in the Quarters (with Fredrick McKissack, 1994)

The Dark-Thirty: Southern Tales of the Supernatural (1992)

Madam C. J. Walker: Self-Made Millionaire (with Fredrick McKissack, 1992)

Sojourner Truth: Ain't I a Woman? (with Fredrick McKissack, 1992)

Carter G. Woodson: The Father of Black History (with Fredrick McKissack, 1992)

W. E. B. DuBois (with Fredrick McKissack, 1990)

A Long Hard Journey: The Story of the Pullman Porter (with Fredrick McKissack, 1989)

Flossie & the Fox (1986)

When Do You Talk to God? Prayers for Small Children (1986)

Paul Laurence Dunbar: A Poet to Remember (1984)

McKissack's Major Literary Awards

2000 Carter G. Woodson Honor Book
2000 Coretta Scott King Author Honor Book
  Black Hands, White Sails: The Story of African-American Whalers

1997 Coretta Scott King Author Honor Book
  Rebels against Slavery: American Slave Revolts

1995 Coretta Scott King Author Award
1995 Orbis Pictus Honor Book
  Christmas in the Big House, Christmas in the Quarters

1995 Coretta Scott King Author Honor Book
  Black Diamond: The Story of the Negro Baseball Leagues

1993 Boston Globe–Horn Book Nonfiction Award
1993 Coretta Scott King Author Honor Book
  Sojourner Truth: Ain't I a Woman?

1993 Carter G. Woodson Book Award
  Madam C. J. Walker: Self-Made Millionaire

1993 Coretta Scott King Author Award
1993 Newbery Honor Book
  The Dark-Thirty: Southern Tales of the Supernatural

1992 Carter G. Woodson Outstanding Merit Book
  Carter G. Woodson: The Father of Black History

1991 Carter G. Woodson Outstanding Merit Book
  W. E. B. DuBois

1990 Carter G. Woodson Outstanding Merit Book
1990 Coretta Scott King Author Award
  A Long Hard Journey: The Story of the Pullman Porter

Through her teaching, she has tried to inspire her students with her own love of literature.

McKissack has also written highly praised fictional tales with realistic black characters as well as stories about country mice and city mice. Her stories are notable for their depiction of human emotion. Her tales are often inspired by her childhood in the South.

Patricia McKissack's fiction and nonfiction are charged with a sense of pride and history.

McKissack seems to have lived up to Kennedy's challenge, giving something back to society and helping to shape a better one.

> *"Writing has allowed us to do something positive with our experiences, although some of our experiences have been very negative. We try to enlighten, to change attitudes, to form new attitudes—to build bridges with books."*

WHERE TO FIND OUT MORE ABOUT PATRICIA MCKISSACK

BOOKS

Kovacs, Deborah, and James Preller. *Meet the Authors and Illustrators: 60 Creators of Favorite Children's Books Talk about Their Work.* Vol. 2. New York: Scholastic, 1993.

McElmeel, Sharron L. *100 Most Popular Children's Authors: Biographical Sketches and Bibliographies.* Englewood, Colo.: Libraries Unlimited, 1999.

WEB SITES

BIOGRAPHY WRITER'S WORKSHOP WITH PATRRICIA AND FREDRICK MCKISSACK
http://teacher.scholastic.com/writewit/biograph/index.htm
To learn from the authors who write a biography

PATRICIA MCKISSACK HOME PAGE
http://www.patriciamckissack.com/
To read information about the author and her works

MCKISSACK IS A MEMBER OF THE METHODIST CHURCH. SHE HAS INCORPORATED RELIGIOUS THEMES INTO SEVERAL BOOKS, INCLUDING *WHEN DO YOU TALK TO GOD? PRAYERS FOR SMALL CHILDREN.*

Milton Meltzer

Born: May 8, 1915

For more than four decades, Milton Meltzer has used his books to share his ideals with young people. He is the author of almost one hundred books, most of them for children and young adults. In each book, he passes on his deep convictions about social justice.

Milton Meltzer was born in Worcester, Massachusetts, in 1915. His parents were Jewish immigrants from Austria. As a child, Milton saw how hard it was for immigrants to adjust to life in the United States. He watched his parents try to fit in with American society. This involved putting their past and their Jewish culture behind them. After he grew up, Meltzer sorely regretted that his parents had not shared their heritage with him.

AMONG MELTZER'S MANY BIOGRAPHIES ARE THE LIFE STORIES OF U.S. PRESIDENT THOMAS JEFFERSON, EXPLORER FERDINAND MAGELLAN, POET WALT WHITMAN, AND AUTHOR MARK TWAIN.

At age five, Milton went to Worcester's Union Hill School. He loved learning to read, write, and do arithmetic. When he was in high school, he held various jobs to make money for his family. He delivered newspapers and milk and worked on a loading dock.

Meltzer attended Columbia University in New York City from 1932 to 1936. At that time, the country was suffering through the economic hard times of the Great Depression. To help people out, the U.S. government established many employment programs. One such program was the Works Projects Administration (WPA). Meltzer worked as a writer for the WPA from 1936 to 1939.

A Selected Bibliography of Meltzer's Work

Herman Melville (2006)

The Cotton Gin (2004)

Hear That Train Whistle Blow!: How the Railroad Changed the World (2004)

The Day the Sky Fell: A History of Terrorism (2002)

Driven from the Land: The Story of the Dust Bowl (2000)

Langston Hughes (1997)

Frederick Douglass, in His Own Words (editor, 1995)

Slavery: A World History (1993)

The Bill of Rights: How We Got It and What It Means (1990)

Black Americans: A History in Their Own Words, 1619–1983 (editor, 1984)

The Jewish Americans: A History in Their Own Words, 1650–1950 (editor, 1982)

The Chinese Americans (1980)

Never to Forget: The Jews of the Holocaust (1976)

Taking Root: Jewish Immigrants in America (1976)

Brother, Can You Spare a Dime? The Great Depression 1929–1933 (1969)

A Light in the Dark: The Life of Samuel Gridley Howe (1964)

Meltzer's Major Literary Awards

2001 Laura Ingalls Wilder Award

1998 Carter G. Woodson Book Award
    Langston Hughes

1983 Boston Globe-Horn Book Nonfiction Honor Book
    The Jewish Americans: A History in Their Own Words, 1650–1950

1981 Carter G. Woodson Book Award
    The Chinese Americans

1976 Boston Globe-Horn Book Nonfiction Honor Book
    Never to Forget: The Jews of the Holocaust

During World War II (1939–1945), Meltzer served in the U.S. Army Air Force. In 1941, he married Hilda Balinky. They eventually had two daughters, Jane and Amy.

After the war, Meltzer began a fifteen-year career in public relations. For most of that time, he handled public relations for companies in the pharmaceutical industry. This involved writing articles for the public about medicines and drug companies. In 1960, he began working as an editor at Science and Medicine Publishing Company in New York City.

For years, Meltzer had been writing for adults. Then one day, his daughter Jane urged him to write something for kids. He gave in to her wishes, publishing *A Light in the Dark: The Life of Samuel Gridley Howe* in 1964. (Howe was a reformer in the 1800s who fought to improve conditions for blind people.) This book marked the beginning of Meltzer's career as a children's book author. In 1968, he left his editorial position to become a full-time writer.

> *"I try to make readers understand that history isn't only what happens to us. History is what we make happen. Each of us. All of us."*

In all of his books, Meltzer reveals aspects of poverty, injustice, and other social ills in America. He often uses primary sources such as first-person accounts, letters, and diaries. Slavery, child labor,

MELTZER MADE $23.86 A WEEK WHEN HE WORKED FOR THE WPA IN THE 1930s. AT THAT TIME, GOODS AND SERVICES COST MUCH LESS THAN THEY DO TODAY, SO $23.86 A WEEK WAS A COMFORTABLE SALARY.

discrimination, crime, women's rights—all these subjects come to life for young readers in Meltzer's books.

Meltzer's own life experiences inspire much of his work. He wrote about the hardships of the Great Depression in *Brother, Can You Spare a Dime? The Great Depression, 1929–1933*. His family's struggles led him to write *Taking Root: Jewish Immigrants in America*. Today, Meltzer is still writing in his home in New York City.

> *"All my writing comes out of my convictions. I've never had to write about anything I didn't believe in."*

WHERE TO FIND OUT MORE ABOUT MILTON MELTZER

BOOKS

Pendergast, Tom, and Sara Pendergast, eds. *St. James Guide to Young Adult Writers*. 2nd ed. Detroit: St. James, 1999.

Silvey, Anita, ed. *The Essential Guide to Children's Books and Their Creators*. Boston: Houghton Mifflin Company, 2002.

Ward, Martha E., ed., et al. *Authors of Books for Young People*. 3rd ed. Metuchen, N.J.: Scarecrow Press, 1990.

WEB SITES

CBC MAGAZINE
http://www.cbcbooks.org/cbcmagazine/perspectives/choosing_award-winning_nonfict.html
For a perspective from the author on awards for nonfiction writing

WORCESTER AREA WRITERS
http://www.wpi.edu/Academics/Library/Archives/WAuthors/meltzer/
For a biography and a list of works by the author

MELTZER'S FIRST BOOK WAS PUBLISHED IN 1956. IT WAS AN ADULT BOOK HE COAUTHORED WITH AFRICAN AMERICAN WRITER LANGSTON HUGHES CALLED *A PICTORIAL HISTORY OF THE NEGRO IN AMERICA*.

Eve Merriam

Born: July 19, 1916
Died: April 11, 1992

Eve Merriam didn't choose to be a poet. Instead, poetry chose her. As a child and as an adult, Merriam felt that writing poetry was one of the most important things in her life. During a successful career that spanned more than four decades, Merriam wrote hundreds of poems for children and grown-ups alike. She wrote about serious subjects and silly subjects, from poverty and crime to vanilla ice cream and umbrellas. Merriam also created picture books and nonfiction works for kids as well as books and plays for adults.

Eve Merriam was born on July 19, 1916, in Philadelphia, Pennsylvania. Her mother and father were Russian immi-

MERRIAM WAS ALSO A GIFTED PLAYWRIGHT. HER PLAYS, SOME OF WHICH SHE PRODUCED AND DIRECTED, HAVE BEEN PERFORMED ON BROADWAY AND IN THEATERS ACROSS THE COUNTRY.

grants. They owned a dress shop in Philadelphia, which sparked Eve's lifelong interest in fashion. The youngest of four children, Eve had two older sisters and an older brother.

Growing up, Eve learned to love the sound of poetry spoken aloud. She was drawn to its rhythm and rhyme. Eve loved the way every single word in a poem is important. Some of the first poems Eve read aloud were printed in her local newspaper. These poems encouraged her to create her own verses, and she composed one of her first poems when she was just seven.

Eve wrote about everything and anything. One of her early poems was about a birch tree

A Selected Bibliography of Merriam's Work

Low Song (2001)

On My Street (2000)

Emma Lazarus Rediscovered (1998)

Bam, Bam, Bam (1995)

Quiet, Please (1993)

The Singing Green: New and Selected Poems for All Seasons (1992)

A Poem for a Pickle: Funnybone Verses (1989)

You Be Good & I'll Be Night: Jump-on-the-Bed Poems (1988)

Blackberry Ink: Poems (1985)

Finding a Poem (1970)

It Doesn't Always Have to Rhyme (1964)

There Is No Rhyme for Silver (1962)

A Gaggle of Geese (1960)

The Real Book about Franklin D. Roosevelt (1952)

> *"I find it difficult to sit still when I hear poetry or read it out loud. I feel a tingling feeling all over, particularly in the tips of my fingers and in my toes, and it just seems to go right from my mouth all the way through my body."*

outside her window. A line of the poem read, "May my life be like the birch tree reaching upward to the sky."

As an adult, Merriam moved to New York City and began a career as a writer. She wrote advertisements, radio scripts, feature stories, and fashion articles. At the same time, she continued to pen her poems.

Her first success as a poet came in 1946. That year, Merriam won an award from Yale University for the most promising young poet. Yale also published her first book, a collection of adult poems called *Family Circle*.

In 1952, Merriam wrote her first children's book—a biography titled *The Real Book about Franklin D. Roosevelt*. After her two sons were born, Merriam became interested in creating other quality books for kids. Her first picture book, *A Gaggle of Geese*, was published in 1960. With its use of wild and wacky words, the book demonstrated Merriam's love for the English language.

In 1962, Merriam published *There Is No Rhyme for Silver*, her first collection of children's poetry. Kids loved Merriam's poems, and more volumes of verse quickly followed.

FOR A WHILE, MERRIAM HAD HER OWN WEEKLY SHOW ON
A NEW YORK CITY RADIO STATION, IN WHICH SHE DISCUSSED MODERN POETRY.

Over the years, Merriam wrote more than twenty poetry books for children. Along the way, she built a reputation as one of the best children's poets of her time. Merriam's poems are fun to read, and they create a love of reading and language in kids.

On April 11, 1992, Merriam died of cancer. Her poems and picture books live on, however. Today, children everywhere continue to enjoy Merriam's amazing work.

> *"As far back as I can remember, I have been intrigued by words: their sound, sight, taste, smell, touch, for it has always seemed to me that they appeal to all the senses."*

WHERE TO FIND OUT MORE ABOUT EVE MERRIAM

BOOKS

Berger, Laura Standley, ed. *Twentieth-Century Young Adult Writers.* 1st ed. Detroit: St. James Press, 1994.

Sutherland, Zena. *Children and Books.* New York: Addison Wesley Longman, 1997.

WEB SITE

THE AMERICAN ACADEMY OF POETS
http://www.poets.org/poet.php/prmPID/159
To learn more about Eve Merriam's life and work

WHILE MERRIAM WAS IN COLLEGE, SHE SLEPT WITH A COPY OF HER FAVORITE BOOK OF POETRY UNDERNEATH HER PILLOW TO MAKE SURE THAT NO ONE STOLE THE BOOK.

A. A. Milne

Born: January 18, 1882
Died: January 31, 1956

A. A. Milne spent most of his career as a writer producing plays. Most of his plays, written for an adult audience, were first performed in the 1920s in theaters in London, England, and New York City. Even though Milne wrote only four children's books, he is best known for his work as a children's author. He wrote *Winnie-the-Pooh* and *The House at Pooh Corner.* The characters in these books went on to become favorites of children and adults throughout the world.

Alan Alexander (A. A.) Milne was born on January 18, 1882, in London. Alan's father owned a private school near their home. Alan attended school there until he won a scholarship to the Westminster School. He then went on to Cambridge University.

MILNE HAD THE HABIT OF SOLVING CROSSWORD
PUZZLES IN THE EVENING AFTER DINNER.

A. A. Milne was a very good student and worked hard. He studied mathematics at the university. He was the editor of the college magazine.

Milne graduated from college in 1903 and began his career as a writer. He became known for humorous essays and plays. His essays were published in a British humor magazine called *Punch*. In 1906, he was offered a job as an assistant editor at *Punch*. He worked at the magazine for eight years.

In 1913, Milne married Dorothy de Selincourt. He joined the British army when World War I (1914–1918) began. While he was training for service in the army, Milne wrote his first play, *Wurzel-Flummery*. By 1920, Milne had completed one book and several plays. He was very successful and made money from his writing. Milne's only son, Christopher Robin, was born in 1920.

"A pen-picture of a child which showed it as loving, grateful, and full of thought for others would be false to the truth; but equally false would be a picture which insisted on the brutal egotism of the child, and ignored the physical beauty which softens it."

Milne wrote his first children's book while taking a break from writing plays. A friend was starting a magazine for children and asked him to write a few verses for the publication. As Milne watched his son play, he wrote the verses. The poems

DISNEY HAS PRODUCED SEVERAL MOVIES OF THE POOH STORIES.

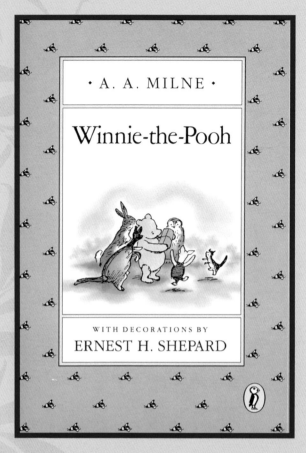

A Selected Bibliography of Milne's Work

The House at Pooh Corner (1928)
Now We Are Six (1927)
Winnie-the-Pooh (1926)
When We Were Very Young (1924)

were published in Milne's first children's book, *When We Were Very Young.*

In 1926, Milne published the first of two books of short stories about Winnie-the-Pooh. His book *The House at Pooh Corner* was published in 1928. He also wrote another book of poetry, *Now We Are Six,* in 1927.

Milne's poetry and short stories were about his son and his own memories of childhood. "My father was a creative writer and so it was precisely because he was not able to play with his small son that his longings sought and found satisfaction in another direction," Christopher Milne later noted. "He wrote about him instead."

The children's books that Milne wrote helped him to relive his own childhood. A. A. Milne continued to write essays, novels, and poetry until his death on January 31, 1956.

> *"It has been my good fortune as a writer that what I have wanted to write has for the most part proved to be saleable."*

❧

WHERE TO FIND OUT MORE ABOUT A. A. MILNE

BOOKS

Toby, Arlene. *A. A. Milne: Author of Winnie-the-Pooh.* Chicago: Children's Press, 1995.

Ward, S. *Meet A. A. Milne.* New York: PowerKids Press, 2001.

Wheeler, Jill. *A. A. Milne.* Edina, Minn.: Abdo & Daughters, 1992.

WEB SITES

POOH CORNER
http://www.pooh-corner.com/biomilne.html
For a biographical sketch of A. A. Milne and information on the Pooh series and characters

WINNIE THE POOH.COM
http://www.winniethepooh.co.uk/author.html
To read a biographical sketch of A. A. Milne, descriptions of Pooh and his friends, and stories and poems by the author

———

WINNIE-THE-POOH HAS BEEN TRANSLATED INTO FRENCH, SPANISH, AND SEVERAL OTHER LANGUAGES.

INDEX